THE ART & TECHNIQUE OF USING FLOWER ESSENCES

Effectively working with Nature's Healing Grace

The Art & Technique

of using

Flower Essences

Effectively working with Nature's Healing Grace

by Cynthia Athina Kemp Scherer

Desert Alchemy Editions
Tucson, Arizona, USA

Published by Desert Alchemy Editions
P.O. Box 44189, Tucson, AZ 85733, USA

Photograph, cover and book design by Camillo Scherer

ISBN 0-9659900-1-X

Library of Congress Catalog Number 2002190100

Printed in the United States of America

9   8   7   6   5   4   3   2   1

*This book is dedicated to all those
who seek the support of nature.
May you experience deep joy
and delight as you allow
the essence of nature to uncover
the essence of you!*

CONTENTS

FOREWORD 11

CHAPTER 1

Effectively Working with Nature's Healing Grace 15

CHAPTER 2

The Core Issue 21

CHAPTER 3

Intuition 29

CHAPTER 4

Inner Awareness 33
    Emotional Awareness 34
    Contemplation 35

CHAPTER 5

Flower Essence Therapy 39
    The Scope of Flower Essences 40
    The Five-Step Process 46
    Documenting the Process 49
    What to Document 50

CHAPTER 6

Step One: Invocation – The Foundation of Healing 53
    Your Higher Self 54
    Other People 55
    The Angelic Realm 56

Qualities 57

Exercise: Creating Your Healing Support Team 60

CHAPTER 7

Step Two: Defining Your Intention 63

Part One: Identify Your Needs 64

Part Two: Find the Harmonizing Qualities 67

Part Three: Write Down Your Intention 68

CHAPTER 8

Step Three: Selecting the Flower Essences 71

How Many Essences to Use 73

Using a Pendulum 75

What Kind of Pendulum to Use 77

The Mechanics of Using a Pendulum 79

Exercise: Establishing your Pendulum Language 80

Selecting Flower Essences with a Pendulum 82

Challenges & Solutions 85

Using Intuitive Impression 87

How to Use Intuitive Impression 89

Using Flower Cards 91

The Attraction/Aversion Method 92

Flower Card Draw 94

The Flower Power Circle 95

Visual Attunement 97

Using Flower Cards in Groups 99

Using Kinesiology 101

Finger Positions if You are Right Handed 102

Finger Positions if You are Left Handed 103

Testing the Affirmative and Negative Response 104

Selecting Flower Essences with Kinesiology 105

Using a Cross-reference 108

CHAPTER 9

Step Four: Using Flower Essences 111
How Long to Use a Flower Essence 112
How Do you Determine the Cycle Time? 116
Finding the Cycle Time Using a Pendulum 117
Finding the Cycle Time Using Intuitive Impression 119
Finding the Cycle Time Using Kinesiology 119
Using the "Default" Cycle Time 119

CHAPTER 10

Step Five: Evaluating the Effects 121
Evaluating the Effects During and After
Using the Flower Essences 123
Sample Documentation of a Flower Essence Session 126
Sample Documentation of a Follow Up Evaluation 128

CHAPTER 11

Selecting Flower Essences for Yourself 131
A Few Challenges and Resolutions 132
Self-confidence 132
Remembering to Ask for Support 133
Honesty with Yourself 134
Too Close to See 136
Taking too Much Responsibility 137
Reality Check 137

CHAPTER 12

Flower Essence Support Circles 139
A Few Challenges and Resolutions 140
Having Good Boundaries 140
Support in Consciousness 142
A Sense of Balance - Giving & Receiving Support 145

Supportive Feedback 147

Honesty with Yourself and Your Friends 148

How to Create a Flower Essence Support Circle 149

The Participants 149

The Roles 150

When to Meet 151

A Flower Essence Support Circle Format 152

CHAPTER 13

Selecting Flower Essences for Others 155

What is Motivating You? 158

Children 160

Pets & Animals 162

Working with Plants 164

CHAPTER 14

Working with a Flower Essence Practitioner 165

Feedback to Give Your Flower Essence Practitioner 168

Common Questions asked of
Flower Essence Practitioners 168

APPENDIX A

The Flower Essence Journal 173

APPENDIX B

Flower Essences Mentioned in this Book 187

APPENDIX C

Resources 189

FOREWORD

The secret of the wisdom of the ancients is "that which is most powerful is that which is most subtle." Unfortunately, we today are not generally geared to notice the subtle.

This remarkable little book is designed to lead us step by common sense step into a working relationship with the subtle realms where the power of healing resides. I have no doubt that such a relationship is what we need and that now is when we need it.

Healing, I have come to believe, is about recovering and integrating parts of ourselves that were cut off and lost from awareness. Healing is about cracking the ego, the way of being that we cling to at the moment, in order to allow a new way of being to emerge. It is about letting go the residues of the past that we hold on to desperately, so we can step freely into a broader consciousness. Flower essences are gentle, subtle, and yet powerful tools for easing us through these steps.

Flower essences have been called "psychotherapy in a bottle" – and while this is not precisely correct (psychotherapy at its best can offer a crucial relationship element that can't be bottled) – there is some truth in it.

The point is that the pace of the last century's psychotherapeutic process is no longer brisk enough for the changes that we need and are experiencing today. Healing is undergoing a "quickening." Healing is becoming the fundamental process that pulsates through our veins, the direction and drive that underlies our lives. We are destined to learn to heal with more and more facility and alacrity.

Flower essences are beginning to emerge as the logical and inevitable medium for this crescendo of healing activity. Inevitable because the flowers surround us, embodying graphically and energetically the shades of consciousness that we experience internally, beckoning us to enter and pass through them on our accelerated flight toward wholeness.

When my children and I built a cabin on ancestral land in the Carolinas, we hacked away at the annoying tangles of invasive wisteria. A few months later, in my garden in the Bronx, I found my flowerbeds and apple tree taken over (to my amazement) by the telltale purple of wisteria flowers. Pushing aside my frustration, I gave in to curiosity and consulted the Encyclopaedia of Flower Remedies. "Fear of intimacy, opens the heart to receive and give unconditional love." Humbling, and accurate. In an hour I had the blossoms floating on water in full sun. And yes, it did the job.

Our work is only to open up and receive the help.

Which brings me back to the genius of Cynthia's book. She starts by reminding us that there is help to be had – something we all forget. I like to say in lectures that there is a serious unemployment problem in the celestial realms. Beings of light killing time (if time exists there) – sitting around a card table playing Hearts, perhaps? Waiting for one of us down here to ask so that they can help.

Then Cynthia talks in simple terms about clarifying our intention. What is the healing challenge that we are facing at this moment? Each of these steps is so sensible, so obvious, how does it escape our attention?

I think the answer is that we are fixated on the physical. We follow a process if it involves tangible materials and changes. If it transpires on the inner planes, we get distracted and lose sight of it. Then it, the process, loses momentum and fades away.

The simple steps that Cynthia articulates with such consistent clarity provide us something to hang onto – a routine that helps us keep the healing process in view, keep it alive and moving – so that the power of the subtle can be successfully harnessed.

Though the routine she offers can amplify the power of flower essences many fold, its value goes well beyond that. Attending methodically to this little system of shepherding healing along actually trains us to do it in other settings as well. Settings where there may be no flower remedies involved.

Asking for help, articulating your intention, selecting your healing measure, remedy, or action, implementing what you chose, and evaluating the effects. These are the steps that must become second nature to us as we make healing our way of life – so that we are always opening to what we had not seen, embracing and integrating it, expanding our identity, and moving into new ways of being. It is through this process that we will leave behind the violence, the greed, and the misery that seems to threaten to engulf the world at this time.

I am sure that you can use Cynthia's steps to work with other flower essences besides the powerful ones she brings us from the desert. I suspect that the day will come when we will even use her approach without the flower remedies themselves – perhaps merely invoking the image of the flower, or the memory of its fragrance.

Meanwhile, I urge you to start by using them as they are. Avail yourself of this amazing tool for healing and transformation. You will be thrilled, delighted, and enormously benefited.

Rudolph Ballentine, MD
Author, *Radical Healing*
Chief Medical Advisor, Olive Leaf Wholeness Center

March 2002
New York City

Chapter 1

⁓

EFFECTIVELY WORKING WITH NATURE'S HEALING GRACE

Flowers are sunshine, food,
and medicine to the soul.
⁓ Luther Burbank

THE CURATIVE POWER OF NATURE has always been a reference point for healing. Since ancient times we have turned to nature to feed and heal our bodies. Even today's scientists study plants and herbs trying to imitate their composition in the laboratory to create new pharmaceutical drugs.

But the help that is available to us through nature is more profound than we usually recognize or even imagine. Nature can be an invaluable support to feed our soul, soothe and heal our deepest spiritual and emotional wounds, and inspire us in our journey of learning and evolving in consciousness.

Most of us remember the moments of sweet peace and calm we have experienced in the midst of nature. Our most regenerating and relaxing vacations are usually the ones that are planned around spending time in nature. We may go to the beach to relish the sun and water or go hiking and camping in the forest to relax, regroup, and find inspiration for our lives. Our worries and cares quickly take a back seat to the magnificence of the landscape, the beauty of a mountain view, or the respite of a shade tree. In this way, nature is an anchor point that helps us connect with our inner stillnes and hopefully with our own inner truth.

Nature is a whole realm of consciousness with which we can communicate and interact, and from which we can learn and receive support. To effectively access nature's aid for our evolutionary journey, we must consciously establish a relationship with her. As with any relationship, intimacy with nature takes time. It is a cultivating process that demands and deserves attention.

By consciously inviting nature into our lives, we can enjoy a more balanced inner state, no matter what the events of our lives bring. And isn't a peaceful and balanced inner state a thing to cherish?

Many of us cannot go outside into nature every time we are faced with challenges in our daily lives. Some of us long for a life that keeps us closer to nature, yet our daily circumstances prohibit it. Fortunately, there is a way to bring the support of nature into our lives in a simple and effective manner.

Since the early times of human history, flowers have always stood out as a magnetic display, drawing our attention. We use flowers to show respect, to comfort and soothe, to demonstrate our feelings, and to show that we care. Flowers have always been present in spiritual ceremonies and in every celebration of the important times in our lives.

Many ancient cultures, aware of the healing grace of nature that "flows" through flowers, have used the infusion of flowers in water to promote emotional and spiritual harmony, and even to impact physical healing. These flower infusions, also known as flower essences, are a co-creation of nature and humanity.

They are the energetic imprints of flowers that are captured in water and united with the conscious blessings of the person making the essence. They are called essences because they do not contain the physical components of the flower, but rather its subtle energetic presence.

Different aspects of plants support us with various aspects of our healing and evolution. We use herbal preparations, made from physical parts of plants, to help us with physical body needs. When we want to address aspects of our consciousness, we can use the essence of a flower to help us.

Dr. Rudolf Ballentine, in his excellent book *Radical Healing*, wrote:[1]

> *If you think about the flower and how it relates to the plant, it is analogous to our nervous system on the physical level and to our consciousness on a more subtle level. The flower is the blossoming of the plant – the emergence of its true nature. The complexity, beauty, and uniqueness of the plant is made manifest in the flower. Similarly, with us it is our consciousness, our awareness, that is our flowering. A disorder in your consciousness can often be helped with a remedy from the flower that corresponds to it.*

Using flower essences is a way to consciously connect with the healing and supportive power of nature. It is a way to assist our healing journey and cultivate an inner support system as we evolve in consciousness. Nature can also help us to understand our own inner nature. Different plants can give us a way to understand what we are feeling and connect more fully with our spiritual selves.

---

1   *Radical Healing*, Dr. Rudolf Ballentine, Harmony Books, 1999.

To illustrate this, let's consider one of the most magnificent plants of the Sonoran Desert: the saguaro cactus. You have probably seen old western films that have giant, straight cacti poking up out of the earth in the landscape. The Sonoran Desert, where these cacti are found, has a landscape that is very horizontal. Flat, uninterrupted expanses draw the eye to the horizon. The saguaro cacti stand like sentinels and pull our eyes heavenward. Saguaro's flower essence helps us to solidly connect with what we can call our vertical connection to spirit. It helps us to find that the wisdom and answers we seek reside inside ourselves. When this wisdom is found within ourselves, we have the confidence to know that no matter how difficult our life seems, we can go on, we can survive.

Another Sonoran Desert plant, the staghorn cholla cactus, has many cylindrical stem joints which are all of varying lengths and grow in many directions. When you first see this large, shrub-like cactus, the impression is one of disorganization. As a flower essence this cactus helps us after a time of disorganization in our lives. Transformational experiences require that we are "torn up" and our perspectives and cherished ways of perceiving life are shaken up. There comes a point in a transformational experience when we need to be put back together again, hopefully in a new way. Staghorn Cholla flower essence helps us when we are reintegrating after a time of transformation. It supports us in having faith in our innate capacity for self-ordering, helping us pull ourselves back into a semblance of inner order that is in alignment with our soul purpose.

In this age of rapid and deep transformation, flower essences can be a tremendous aid for emotional, mental, and spiritual consciousness. Many therapists have told me that their clients who use flower essences process and resolve issues at a more rapid pace than those who do not.

While flower essences have been used in many countries since the 1930's as an inexpensive way to address healing at the consciousness level, they have only become known here in the United States in the last twenty-five or so years.

Flower essence therapy is inherently self-empowering, inexpensive, simple and safe. Flower essences are safe to use for self-help because if you take a flower essence that you don't need, nothing will happen. This is not true of pharmaceutical drugs or even herbal preparations, where the dosage and some combinations can be toxic. Since flower essences are a vibrational preparation, they will not interact adversely with natural or synthetic drugs or medications.

In my previous book, *The Alchemy of the Desert*,[1] I described in detail how flower essences work and I included in-depth information about one hundred thirty-five desert flower essences. You can refer to it for further information.

Many people are now aware of how powerfully flower essences can help them. At a time when "natural" products are becoming an increasingly complex industry, it is comforting to know that an inexpensive, hand-made flower essence can provide a simple way for us to receive nature's healing grace.

The challange, however, is how to effectively select them. Almost every day I am asked, "How can I find the best flower essence to use for myself? There is so much going on in my life; where do I start?" Or, folks tell me, "I read about the different flower essences and I think I need them all! How do I choose?"

The purpose of this book is to present a simple, comprehensive, and self-empowering method for selecting and using flower essences and evaluating their effects.

---

1   *The Alchemy of the Desert*, Cynthia Athina Kemp Scherer, Desert Alchemy Editions, 1997.

In the following chapters, I present a five-step method for this purpose. This method is both an art and a technique. Like any art form, once you learn the technique you will be able to create an inspired result. My purpose is to help you pinpoint your core need, to present several ways to select flower essences, and to give you a simple method for recognizing and evaluating their effects.

The five-step process can help you understand your inner reality: your feelings; your thoughts; old thought patterns that may no longer be useful; and your relationship with spirit and soul.

The five-step process that I share in this book began to unfold spontaneously when I was guided by an inner prompting to begin making and using flower essences. I have been using this same process, both for myself and in my practice as a flower essence practitioner, for more than eighteen years. Even today, when I select flower essences in this way, I am amazed at the accuracy of the indicated essences and what they teach my clients and myself.

When selecting flower essences, I like to address the underlying core issue, rather than what appears on the surface. Core issues are usually rooted deep within our relationship with spirit and our soul. By focusing at this level, we can still address any mundane issues or problems, but we do it by harmonizing the cause of the disharmony.

The approach I use for selecting flower essences focuses on creating harmony within us, rather than focusing on the symptoms, or the disharmony. The discomforting manifestations we experience, which can be attitudinal, emotional, physical, or spiritual in nature, are there to attract our attention to something deeper. Flower essences can help us see what is beneath the attention-grabbing discomfort and can help create a state of harmony, which restores us to balance.

I think it is of utmost importance to honor what our soul is telling us. When we include our feelings and intuition as equal partners with our intellect, we can hear the needs of the soul. The five-step process supports us in recognizing and honoring our intuition. When we select flower essences in this way, we have the opportunity to become adept at using our intuition.

Asking for help is of the utmost importance when selecting flower essences. When we invoke the spiritual support that is available to us, we receive a high quality of results. The five-step process presented here includes a way to ask for support.

Many folks try to select flower essences with intuitive methods without first becoming clear what it is that they want to change. When we consciously create an intention, we become self-empowered and an active participant in our healing process. This important aspect is also covered in the following chapters.

Often, when people use flower essences, they have a difficult time recognizing their effects. They report that although they feel better, they are not sure what effect the essences had. The five-step process includes a way for recognizing how the flower essences worked.

Core issues, harmony, partnering intellect with intuition, invocation, and self-empowerment are all key elements in selecting the flower essences that will support you with the greatest success in healing and evolving. The five-step process itself can enhance these qualities in you.

∞

Chapter 2

—

THE CORE ISSUE

The essential is invisible to the eye.
~ St. Exupèry, *The Little Prince*

WE ALL HAVE AN INHERENT healing power within ourselves. It exists within us, whether or not we recognize it. Different life events, often of the painful variety, may awaken our awareness to this inner source. With the aid of flower essences, our awareness can naturally open to our innate healing resource. All we need to have is the desire to access and consciously use our inner healing support.

The process of becoming aware of inner healing support is one of *allowing* and not one of *doing*. Having the attitude that we have to do something can be counter-productive to success. This is a very different attitude than we might have been taught for most things in life. It is not that we have to learn more, but rather that we need to unlearn, to uncover what is already within us.

When I work with flower essences, I like to address the core, or root, of the situation that is causing discomfort or unease. It is easy to see the effects of a situation and become caught up in attempting to deal with them. Yet I have found that what appears to be the "problem" is often just a symptom of a deeper life issue. When we can work at this deeper level we may spend much less time and energy than we would if we were working with a more superficial focus. Often when we work with the core or root of a situation, many of the uncomfortable symptoms that held our attention melt away. Some uncomfortable situations that seemed unrelated often come into harmony and are resolved almost effortlessly once we have addressed the deeper cause.

Often people ask me questions such as the following: "What flower essences would you recommend for depression?" or "What flower essence can I use for anger?" My first response to that kind of question is usually another question. "Why are you depressed?" or "What is it about your anger that is creating a problem?" would be typical queries.

Most of us have been taught to look at our symptoms and find a way to alleviate them. Yet our symptoms are usually the language our soul is using to get us to pay attention to a deeper issue.

When we look for the core of an issue or discomfort, we do not use the symptom as the focal point. It is very easy to get caught up in the "appearance" of the situation that is creating our discomfort. When we focus on the symptom, we are looking at the tip of the proverbial iceberg and ignoring what is under the surface.

What appears at the surface is an alarm, a warning, like a smoke alarm in our home that warns us. All good alarms are obnoxious, and for a good reason. They force us to pull our attention from what we are doing and to urgently deal with something more important. Even though alarms are a nuisance, they are our friends and not the problem.

The real problem is often "invisible to the eye." It is what I call the core, or root, of the issue. Dealing with the core of an issue is key to the success of any form of therapy. Why are some causes invisible to us while others are readily seen? We usually see the cause-effect connection in things that are immediate. For instance, if we hold our hand over a flame and we are burned, we know that the fire was the cause of the burn because the effect was immediate and we get the same results each time we repeat the action. Many of our actions have consequences that are not immediate, and those are the causes that are invisible to the eye.

I like to call flower essences agents of consciousness. They can help us see beyond the apparent to find the essential. Their very nature is essential, as they are the essence, or essential consciousness, of a plant. They help us see our own essence, or essential aspects of ourselves.

If our intention is to have the flower essences address the core, or root, of a situation, we might save ourselves a lot of time spent on dissecting and understanding the symptoms. Symptoms are usually provocative: they draw our attention to the drama of life. They can entrance us by encouraging us to spend a lot of focus on the inessential. What we focus on expands, and the more focus we direct to our symptoms the stronger they can become.

To return to the question above, "What flower essence can I use for anger?", it appears that the focal point of this question is the symptom, which is anger. Anger is fine. It is a feeling that all of us have and need. But what is it about the anger that is creating the discomfort? Are you judging yourself for being angry? Are you expressing your anger in an inappropriate way? Do you feel that your anger takes over and you are out of control? What is underneath the anger that is creating discomfort? When we select flower essences with the intention of finding the core of the discomfort, we will select flower essences that can show us the underlying cause. If we attempt to understand the underlying cause, we can more effectively find harmony with a situation that is creating the discomfort.

While it is possible to effect a change by focusing on our symptoms, it is usually more efficient to address the core issue. However, if you are most comfortable working from the symptom level, it is fine to do so. One way is not more correct than the other, but feedback from many folks who are now using the core issue approach to selecting flower essences suggests that a deepening in consciousness is usually the reward.

> *I have been selecting and using flower essences, both professionally and personally, for the past eight and a half years. However, since I have been using your five-step process, I can't tell you how dramatic a difference it has made for both my clients and myself. I find that I move through my "stuff" much more quickly, and I have more confidence in myself as I move through things. It feels as though I am waking up and becoming more conscious. I have also seen a tremendous difference with the pace at which many of my clients have resolved old issues that had been hanging around for a long time without final resolution.*
>
> ~ A.H., Chicago, IL

Sometimes, to address the cause of our pain or discomfort, we may find ourselves dealing with issues we never thought were related. How does this happen? Sara (not her real name) came to me wanting to deal with her fear of public speaking. She was a university professor and she found this fear extremely debilitating. She had been teaching for about six years and confessed that she was terrified of being in front of her students. This fear had filled her life with stress, almost on a daily basis. She was open to using flower essences, even though she had no experience with them.

Over the period of the next two years, as we selected flower essences every three to four weeks, Sara came face to face with several core issues that at first seemed unrelated. The first issue she had to face was how she relentlessly controlled her husband. Over the next months she learned to let go and allow her partner to be more autonomous.

Then she faced a serious legal problem in which she had been less than honest. She found the courage to face it and tell the truth. The freedom she found after resolving this situation brought her courage to face other issues.

Next, Sara courageously faced the fact that she needed to heal from having been raped as a teenager. In this journey she uncovered a memory she had never been able to face: that she had been sexually abused as a child.

As she worked with resolving her feelings from these intense experiences, she began to accept and forgive herself and a deep feeling of self-love began to awaken within. After only a few months of using the flower essences she had begun to feel more self-confident in front of her classes, but she still had some panic when she had to interact with other university staff or in other public speaking events.

As she resolved the issues that came from having been sexually abused, she became completely comfortable in any public speaking situation and in her interactions with university politics. Although Sara had originally wanted to be more comfortable as a professor, her desire to heal her intense discomfort in the classroom had brought her face to face with other issues that she had ignored, or of which she had been unconscious.

The journey of healing usually leads us to surprising and sometimes uncomfortable places. It requires courage, faith and determination to stay with the process and where it takes us.

To heal and evolve, we have to face things within ourselves that we do not like, that we feel we may never be able to overcome, or that we just do not want to see. None of us wants to be in pain, yet I have come to trust in the discomfort and uneasiness that leads us to seek change and healing. It is the impetus or catalyst for moving out of a stagnant or confining life experience. If we can learn to view discomfort as our friend and ally, we may be able to more quickly activate the healing process when we encounter our discomfort.

There are particular healing journeys that I might not have started if I had known in advance the feelings I would have to face. The depth and intensity of my path was unexpected and painful. Yet once I completed each process and could see the benefits it brought me, I knew that I would not have changed any of them.

We are given the gift of seeing our courage, tenacity, faith and determination as we face each healing opportunity. We experience healing grace in our lives and we find an intimate relationship with our Creator. All these healing experiences bring us a more profound consciousness, which is probably the ultimate goal in our lives.

How do we pinpoint core issues? How can we address the root of an issue? The easiest way is to use our intuition. When we select flower essences using an intuitive method, the flower essences can show us the underlying causes of our discomfort.

Flower Essence Support

If you tend to want to escape from an intense or upsetting situation or awareness, you can use the *Crisis – Desert Emergency Formula*™ to help you keep your attention in the moment, with calm presence and centeredness. We can deal with everything life offers us when we find a place of inner balance.

If you run up against difficulty accepting a painful situation or an uncomfortable healing opportunity and you feel unable to continue, you can use *Saguaro Cactus* flower essence for accessing the determination and tenacity to stay with the process. It helps to remind us that we just need to take one more breath, and experience one more moment, and that all the wisdom we need is right inside us.

Chapter 3

—

INTUITION

*The biggest challenge we face as we select
flower essences is learning to trust our intuition.*

Now that we have established that working with the cause of our discomfort is important, how can we find the core or root of the situation? We can easily address the core of an issue by using an intuitive approach to selecting flower essences. The dictionary defines *intuition* as direct perception of truth, fact, etc., independent of any reasoning process. When we intuit something, we have a keen and often quick insight. Sometimes it feels like a lightning flash, and other times it is a subtle and soft knowing that grows stronger until we either acknowledge or forget it.

All of us have had intuitive insights and ignored them, only to regret it later. At other times we may feel sure that our intuition is telling us something, only to realize later that we were mistaken and the impulse came from a desire within ourselves to make something true.

Intuition is a part of our being. Some of us have developed it more fully than others. Many of us were not taught to recognize and honor our intuition, but it is never too late to start. Developing our intuitive capacity is like exercising a muscle: the more you use it, the stronger it becomes.

Using flower essences helps us to attain an important balance between intuition and logic. When we know something intuitively, we then use our logical mind to verify its truth. It may take a short or long time to "prove" an intuitive hunch, but our logical mind is a great and necessary friend in this process.

When we first open to our intuitive nature, we may feel ungrounded as we explore the process of trusting our intuition. We sometimes have to allow ourselves to do some stupid things in order to learn what is real and what is imagined. This is an important part of learning the difference between intuition and wishful thinking. It's important to keep an open mind, but not let our brains fall out!

Most of us have been taught to honor our mind over our intuition. We want proof; we want to be able to evaluate everything before we take any action so that we will not be disappointed or surprised by life. Yet our intuition is as vitally important a source of information as our mind. Our intuition can supply insights, impressions and hunches that our mind could never have known.

I like to use an intuitive method for selecting flower essences because I want to be able to go beyond what my mind thinks so I can address underlying causes, or the core issues, that are not obvious. As we discussed in the last chapter, often the root of an issue lies in something that is hidden from our minds, something that we are not yet able to see with our rational faculties. There is an ancient Sufi story about a man called Sheik Nasrudin that illustrates the way our minds work.

Sheik Nasrudin was on all fours in the street, searching the ground in front of his house.

A man came upon him and asked, "What are you doing there?"

"I'm looking for my ring," answered Sheik Nasrudin.

"Shall I help you look? Where did you drop it, right here?" the man asked.

"No, I lost it inside my house," said Nasrudin.

"If you lost your ring inside your house, why are you looking for it here in the street?" asked the puzzled man.

"I'm looking here in the street because there is more light," responded Nasrudin.

We look for causes and answers where there is the most light, where we think we will be able to have clarity. Yet many of the answers and clues lie in our subconscious mind, hidden from the light of our intellect. By using an intuitive method for selecting flower essences, we can help bring buried or unconscious causes into the light of understanding. While the intellect is confined to our conscious mind, our intuition has unlimited access to the regions of our subconscious mind.

The attitudes we have determine our reality. The experiences we have had and the interpretations we have made about them color our attitudes and beliefs about ourselves. We may define a situation as a problem, yet with a different interpretation we may see it as a project or an opportunity for growth instead. Understanding our attitudes can sometimes be a difficult job since they influence our way of thinking and perceiving. Because our intuition has the ability to access our subconscious mind, it can lead us to the flower essences that will help us discover the attitudes that are defining our problems.

The process of learning to select flower essences intuitively will enable you to practice using your intuition. As we practice using our intuition, we soon find that our intuition will become an equal partner with our mind. When the two work together as a team, we experience a greater sense of balance in our lives, and situations that might have once intimidated us become easy to handle. When our minds and our intuition are in a balanced state, we have ready tools for understanding ourselves, for making decisions in life, and for experiencing greater peace. If you feel you need support for using and trusting your intuition, you might consider using *Queen of the Night Cactus* flower essence.

We can provide a focus for our intuition and a clear intention for the flower essences to address when we create a methodical foundation. In the next chapters I will lay out a simple process for creating such a foundation.

Flower Essence Support

The flower essence of *Queen of the Night Cactus* helps us to access and honor our intuition by supporting us in going within and allowing the inner world to be a source of richness.

Chapter 4

Inner Awareness

*Perhaps the greatest skill we can master during our lives
is the ability to tune in to our inner state.*

MOST OF US HAVE LIVES THAT are filled with things to do, responsibilities to keep, jobs to fulfill, and other people's needs to satisfy. With all of these compelling attractions our focus is commonly outward, on life situations and other people. We learn very well how to pay attention to the things outside of us and may not have learned how to focus within ourselves.

Even those of us who have been fortunate enough to know how to meditate and contemplate often are swept away in the busy, outer-life events. It takes self-discipline to set aside time each day for meaningful quiet time and contemplation. Often when we stop long enough to be quiet, we find that our minds are still racing at the speed of life.

Flower essences can help us to more easily quiet ourselves and bring respite from the fast pace of life. Many folks have found that by using flower essences over a period of time, they begin to have a more meaningful relationship with their inner self and a deeper relationship with soul and spirit.

One of the gifts of flower essences is the great support they bring us in recognizing and accepting our inner reality. Our intuition, gut feelings, physical sensations, emotions, as well as our thoughts and attitudes can give us a wealth of information about ourselves and the way we interpret the world around us. When we are aware of our inner state, we become adept in handling the situations in our lives gracefully.

How can we clearly focus on our inner reality? Emotional awareness and contemplation are key elements.

Emotional Awareness

What does it mean to be emotionally aware? When we are conscious of what we are feeling and the attitudes we have, we are emotionally aware. When we can distinguish our feelings from the thoughts we have about them, we are emotionally aware.

It is important to be aware of our feelings and attitudes because they are often the underlying cause of many of the discomforts in life. When we are aware of what we are feeling, thinking and believing, we are able to interact with these feelings and thoughts.

Many of us, when we look inside, feel things that we would rather not feel. We become aware of thoughts or beliefs that we would rather not have. It takes a tremendous amount of energy to push away these feelings and thoughts. When we can observe and accept that we have them, we have mastered the first step to creating the reality we want to have.

There is a desert flower essence that is an important foundation for helping us take this necessary first step. It is called the *Emotional Awareness Formula*™. It helps us to move from our mind into the feeling level of awareness. It supports us in perceiving our thoughts and feelings without judging them. It can balance an overly emotional state as well as an overly intellectual one.

The more aware we are of what we are feeling, sensing, and thinking, the more we can create balance and harmony in our lives.

Contemplation

Contemplation is a spiritual practice that can bring meaning and wisdom into our lives. It can help us to penetrate our doubts, our fears and delusions and bring a higher perspective, or divine presence, into the mundane events of life.

The word contemplation is composed of two parts: *con* means *to be with* and *templation* has its roots in the word *temple*. When we contemplate, we go inside our inner temple. Contemplation helps us activate our inner wisdom, or Higher Power. It is a way of asking for divine answers and helps us make decisions guided by grace. Contemplation can help us to be free from a perspective that is controlled purely by objective thought. It facilitates a marriage of our minds with our hearts.

The more we practice contemplation, the more we find meaning in the daily events of our lives. When we are used to contemplating, we naturally pause to find a higher perspective as we live our lives. Contemplation is essential for selecting flower essences. It helps us understand what kind of support we are seeking as we use the flower essences. Some folks like to have fifteen minutes each day for contemplating. Others use contemplation at any time when they need inner support.

How do we contemplate? There are three easy steps. If you want, you can use the *Saguaro-Queen Formula*™ to help you with the practice of contemplation. Just use four drops of this essence before you start to contemplate. To contemplate, set aside a time in which you will not be interrupted. It might be ten min-utes or even longer if you wish.

1. Choose a subject for contemplation.

It can be an event that you experienced today or at some other time. It might be a relationship that you want to have more insight about. Or, you might want to contemplate something you have heard that intrigues you, and about which you want further understanding. You might want to contemplate your day: what happened or didn't happen, and why you responded the way you did in each situation. No-tice what you feel without judging yourself. Allow yourself to be purely an observer, just for now. Allow yourself pure feeling.

2. Consider it with your mind.

Engage your mind by asking a few questions about the sub-ject, such as the following: What does this mean to me? How can I understand this? What does this situation remind me of? What do I feel about this? Embrace the subject by quiet consideration.

3. Hold it with your heart.

Let your mental focus on the subject go. Now it is time to allow your heart to speak. Calm your mind. Drop into your heart. Ask for the grace to understand with your heart. No-tice what comes up. Sometimes a new awareness arises, or a new perspective or question arises. If you want, you can write down what you have experienced. Don't worry about having to do something with the awareness that has come up. Just let it be.

Contemplation is an important tool that will help us as we learn how to select the flower essences that will help us in the deepest possible way.

Flower Essence Support

The *Emotional Awareness Formula*™ is excellent for helping us tune in to what we are experiencing without being self-judgmental.

The essence that helps us contemplate is the *Saguaro-Queen Formula*™.

Chapter 5

FLOWER ESSENCE THERAPY

All nature forms in general, and flower essences
specifically, provide an avenue for us to receive grace.[1]

FLOWER ESSENCE THERAPY is a term that names the practice of using flower essences in a consistent, purposeful way to experience emotional harmony and spiritual well being. The essences can be used to support or change our emotional attitudes and ways of perceiving. They provide a language that helps us understand our inner world and the ways in which we respond to life and life's situations. Flower essences enhance our spiritual understanding by opening the channels to a direct experience with our soul and spirit.

While many healing modalities focus on the physical aspects of healing, flower essence therapy addresses the emotional and spiritual levels. Healing is a multilevel process that encompasses the whole person, which includes the physical body, the emotions, mental outlook, attitudes and spiritual understanding.

---

1   *The Alchemy of the Desert*, Cynthia Athina Kemp Scherer,
    Desert Alchemy Editions, 1997.

A growing number of health care practitioners now recognize that patients with the best outlook on life and who feel emotionally supported tend to recover faster and have fewer reoccurences of an illness. By incorporating flower essences with other healing therapies, a practitioner can support the client's emotions, attitudes and spiritual awareness.

The Scope of Flower Essences

When we select a flower essence it is usually in response to pain, discomfort or dissatisfaction with the way we perceive the world or ourselves. We are usually faced with one or more of the following when the need arises to use flower essences:

❀ We have been presented with a seemingly difficult problem in our lives.

❀ A change is happening, such as a change in our work, a relationship, our financial situation, our home, etc.

❀ A concept or perspective that was always true for us is no longer valid.

❀ We recognize that things are not the way we would like them to be, and we don't know what or how to change.

❀ We realize that we do not know our life purpose, either spiritually or in a more mundane sense, and we feel a need to define it.

❀ We feel an emptiness inside ourselves and want to understand our spiritual self.

❀ We are having an uncomfortable mental or emotional response to a situation or person.

❀ An uncomfortable emotion has arisen that we don't want to feel.

❀ We are experiencing a feeling that we don't know how to define.

❀ We are acting out behavior that we don't like, but we don't know what to do about it.

❀ A spiritual experience has taken place that we do not understand or that we are having a hard time integrating.

❀ We are in the midst of a transformational experience and we seek support to help us make the journey peacefully.

❀ We see that our perspective is limited and we want change it.

❀ We are dealing with a physical or emotional healing project that seems overwhelming or unending.

❀ We have given up hope and need a change of attitude.

Flower essences have a profound effect in the realm of our emotions, our attitudes, and our ability to focus on, and comprehend, a spiritual meaning for our lives. We can consciously embrace the opportunities that life offers us when we are able to create harmony in these areas of life.

By understanding and accepting our feelings, we gain the freedom to live our lives more consciously, unhindered by knee-jerk reactions to the events of life. Many folks use flower essences to help them heal and resolve emotional issues.

Joan, one of my clients, was going through therapy for recovering from childhood sexual abuse. The healing journey was challenging, and she wanted support for being clear about what she was feeling. One of her main problems was that she needed desperately to have her feelings guide her through this recovery process, but she had learned as a child to distance herself from them.

Her psychologist recommended that she have a series of flower essence consultations with me to accompany the therapy work she was doing. Joan found that the flower essences helped her recognize what she was feeling. They supported her in ceasing the pattern of repressing her feelings before she could recognize them. She began to feel stronger as she embraced her emotions as a supportive aspect of herself, instead of viewing them as a hindrance or an inconvenience. Her psychologist was amazed at how rapidly Joan processed and healed issues once she began using flower essences. The psychologist said that normally it would take most people two or three times longer to resolve similar issues.

In my practice as a flower essence therapist, I have seen people learn to understand and accept their emotions as a natural part of themselves by using flower essences. Many of us have been taught that there are one or more unacceptable emotions. We learned to repress or hide these emotions so that others around us would be more comfortable. Flower essences are playing an enormous role in helping us recognize our emotions and learn how to appropriately express them, even if we were not taught this as children.

I have worked with many men who turned to flower essences to help them identify what they were feeling. In many cultures certain emotions are considered feminine. "Big boys don't cry." Yet many men are searching for a new masculine identity as they realize that feelings are necessary for a healthy and balanced life. Flower essences are helping provide a language for understanding their inner world of feelings.

Many folks now understand that the physical manifestations of symptoms have their roots in emotions and attitudes. They are discovering that flower essences can help us recognize our attitudes and effectively change them, thus providing the release of the cause of certain physical ailments. Different ways of thinking have been ingrained in us by experiences we have had, by societal conditioning and by patterns we have inherited.

Michael, one client of mine, reported the following:"My wife had the flu and I felt myself with the beginnings of a sore throat and a feeling of overall tiredness. I selected flower essences after setting my intention to not get the flu, and I began to take them right away.

"Within a few hours I recognized that I had been thinking, 'Oh, I have to get sick now. It is my turn.' I realized that this thought had been just below the surface of my consciousness; it was there, but I hadn't really noticed it. The flower essences helped me change the feeling of inevitability about having the flu to a decision that I just wasn't going to have it. My symptoms went away within a day."

Perhaps the ultimate experience we seek in life is in finding spiritual meaning in everything we do. One client shared the following story with me about how flower essences brought spiritual insight into a tragic situation.

Her intention was to feel that she was always safe, and she also wanted to be more intuitive. She began using a combination of four flower essences. The day after she began using the essences a close friend of hers died.

She felt overwhelmed by grief and felt that there was no way that she could handle the depth of her grief. The death of her friend brought her the awareness of the vulnerability of life.

43

She said, "After three days of using the flower essences I felt fresh. Something inside me was purified and I began to see the underlying meaning of things." Her perception changed and she began to see a spiritual meaning in the small events of life. She felt that she had more strength and that her friend's death had brought a gift of insight into her life.

Flower essences can also be used when we are just having a bad day. We all have them from time to time. These are the days when everything seems to be strange, challenging, and even punishing. The harder we try, the worse it gets. If we stop and select some flower essences, our whole attitude about the day can change, and the situations that were challenging can become opportunities.

Most people find that flower essences have helped them in one or more of the following areas:

❀ For recognizing and understanding what they are feeling.

❀ For processing painful emotions.

❀ For clarity about what they are experiencing in life.

❀ For all kinds of relationship challenges.

❀ For understanding their life purpose.

❀ For unlocking creativity.

❀ For dealing with the stress and demands of life.

❀ For finding spiritual awareness in the mundane events of life.

❀ In the recovery of past and present traumas.

❀ For clearing or healing issues that seem to stem from a past-life.

❀ For enhancing awareness of the cause of physical symptoms.

❀ To help in a crisis situation, or to heal the effects of a past one.

❀ For support during transformational experiences.

❀ For assisting self-development and personal growth.

❀ For helping in the transitions of life.

❀ For finding self-empowerment, self-love, and self-esteem.

❀ For having an attitude of gratitude.

❀ For just having a great day.

Sometimes we need other healing modalities to help us with a particular issue. Flower essences often help open us up to seek the modality that is a perfect addition to bring new awareness. One client, after using a particular flower essence that helped her to be more in touch with her physical body, reported excitedly that she had begun to have therapeutic massage and was releasing old trauma stored in her body. She said that she had noticed the massage therapist's office about a year previously and had felt drawn to check it out. However, it wasn't until she used that particular flower essence for body awareness that she felt ready to investigate and then begin having therapeutic massage.

Another client wanted flower essence support for a physical condition. She was adamantly opposed to having surgery for a bladder condition which she had had for many years and for which doctors said that a simple surgery was indicated. She was convinced that all surgery was invasive and she didn't want any part of it. After using flower essences for three months, she reported that she was going to have surgery. She said, "You know, it just seems like the right thing to do. I don't know what changed, but it just feels right." She had the surgery and has been completely free of the problem for nearly eight years. She said, "I had hoped that the flower essences would help the condition, and they have, but just not in the way I expected."

The Five-Step Process

Selecting flower essences can be easy when we approach it with five easy steps (see figure 1). The first two steps create the foundation so that the essences we choose address the root or core of what we want. The third step is the selection itself. In the fourth step we use the flower essences. The fifth step shows us how to recognize and evaluate their effects.

The process itself is very simple. The more you use it, the faster and easier it becomes. The first three steps may take one minute, or sometimes it may take half an hour. It depends upon how comfortable you have become with recognizing your inner state and how confident you become with the method you use for selecting the essences.

Whether you are selecting flower essences for yourself, for others, or whether you are working with a therapist or flower essence practitioner, the first two steps create a focal point for the flower essences to address. One person told us:

> Of course, after taking your class, it seems so simple to define my intention before I select the flower essences, but I didn't always do that. I would excitedly look forward to the flower essences themselves and I would go right ahead and select them without clearly defining what I wanted them to work with. Now

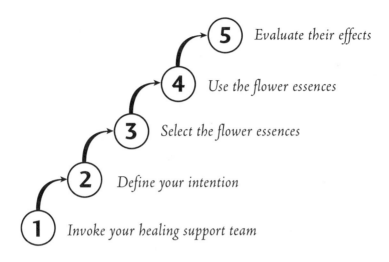

5 — *Evaluate their effects*

4 — *Use the flower essences*

3 — *Select the flower essences*

2 — *Define your intention*

1 — *Invoke your healing support team*

FIG. I – THE FIVE-STEP PROCESS

that I invoke my healing support team and take a few minutes to decide my intention before I select them with intuitive impression, I find an even stronger support from the flower essences.

Another woman, after learning and using the initial two steps before selecting her flower essences, told us:

I have been using flower essences for many years. Since I began using these initial two steps I found that I process issues much easier. Now that I am clearly selecting the flower essences to deal with the root of the situations, I am much calmer as I process and transform. I used to suffer a lot as I went through things and now I don't.

This five-step process evolved spontaneously as I searched for a way to address the core issues, or underlying causes, as I selected flower essences. I saw that by selecting the flower essences in an intuitive way, I could learn from nature. The flowers themselves could show me things about my inner reality of which I had not previously been aware. We have had impressive feedback from professionals and self-help enthusiasts who now use this process.

There are many intuitive ways to select flower essences. A few of them include using a pendulum, kinesiology or muscle testing, intuitive impression, and the flower cards.

Some of us might prefer to use a more left-brained or rational approach to selecting the flower essences. This type of approach might include using a cross-reference. Another way is by studying each essence to understand its harmonizing qualities and the patterns of imbalance it addresses, then matching them up to the needs you perceive by careful observation of yourself. These approaches are perfectly fine. What is most important is to use a method with which you feel comfortable.

Whatever method you choose to use to select flower essences, if you use the initial two steps first, you will be able to select flower essences with greater accuracy and be able to pinpoint whatever lies beneath what seems to be the discomfort or disharmony.

Trusting ourselves to select flower essences is something that we can learn. The process itself and the flower essences we use give us the experiences we need to know ourselves more fully. When we use a system with which we can measure the results, we learn to trust ourselves even more. The five-step process is just such a system.

Documenting the Process

The greatest memory is weaker than the smallest pencil.
~ Anonymous

Working with flower essences is rewarding in many ways. As we use them we necessarily look inside ourselves to recognize and understand our emotions, our thoughts, and our relationship to spirit.

To more easily recognize the effects of the flower essences, it is important to write down your experiences as you use them. When a situation creates discomfort and pushes us to seek the support of flower essences, we think we will never forget the uncomfortable feelings. Yet as we heal, we forget the disharmony that provoked us in the first place. That's a good thing and a sign that we have resolved something. However, if we want to understand the depth of harmony created by the flower essences, we need to provide a reference point from which we can see how far we have come.

If you are selecting flower essences for yourself, documenting your process is usually necessary for creating a foundation for evaluating the effects. When you select flower essences for yourself, you play the role of the observer, or support person, as well as the role of the flower essence user. By writing down your experiences you will be able to refer to the thoughts, feelings, and insights that you had at the time you selected the essences.

Even when we use the support of a friend or professional for selecting flower essences, it is beneficial to write down our experiences. It makes it easier to see any changes and insights in ourselves, as well as to give feedback to our practitioner.

When we write down our experiences, we become clear about our intention and we provide ourselves with a reference point for evaluating the effects of the flower essences we have chosen.

When we journal, or write about our inner reality, we often find ourselves surprised by the feelings that come up. Writing can illuminate our inner state. Even if you are not partial to writing, it is valuable to record at least a few things so that you can have a foundation for evaluating the flower essences' effects. Use a journal or notebook to record the process of selecting your flower essences, or see *Appendix A: The Flower Essence Journal.*

What to Document

The following things are important to write down:

At the time you select flower essences:

❀ The date you select the flower essences.

❀ Your intention for selecting the essences. (Step 2 of the five-step process.)

❀ The name of each flower essence you select.

❀ Any insights about how each flower essence seems to apply to you.

❀ The cycle time.

While you are using the flower essences:

❀ Any insights you have and the date you have them.

❀ General insights about how you are feeling or responding to the events in your life.

❀ If you are reacting to situations and persons differently.

❀ Any insights that might correspond to the patterns of imbalance or harmonizing qualities of each flower essence.

❀ Any other realizations that may or may not seem related to the flower essences you are using.

At the end of the cycle:

❀ The date you evaluate the flower essences' effects.

❀ How often you used the essences.

❀ Any insights and comments about your experiences and any changes you recognize in yourself.

Chapter 6

—

STEP ONE:

INVOCATION –

THE FOUNDATION OF HEALING

You have to do it yourself,
but you can't do it alone.

WE CAN HAVE A HEALING support team at our disposal, twenty-four hours a day, three hundred sixty-five days a year. All we need to do is consciously ask for it. If you want to work most effectively with flower essences, it is essential to consciously invoke a healing support team.

To invoke means to call for with earnest desire, to pray for, to call on a deity, angel or muse for help or protection. If we want to enhance our healing process, we need only to ask for support and help. The only time we do not receive support is when we don't ask for it.

There are several sources to think about when creating a healing support team: your Higher Self; other people; guides and teachers; the angelic realm; and specific qualities. If we want to have the greatest success in taking responsibility for our own healing, we can call upon the support from these sources and create a healing support team that is always available.

Being responsible for our healing process does not mean that we have to figure it all out by ourselves. The paradox is that we have the power and the responsibility to be involved in our healing, but we need to ask for the help and inspiration to experience the harmonizing qualities of healing grace.

We need to use our personal will to create the movement towards harmony. By consciously looking at what we want to change, and by being aware of what we want to experience in its place, we initiate the movement of harmony. We have to do it ourselves, but we cannot do it alone. We ourselves, through our personal will, are the initiators of the healing process. However, we are but one member of a team.

To create an effective and powerful healing support team, it is helpful if you spend a little time contemplating what sort of members you want to include.

Your Higher Self

Perhaps the first member you might want to invoke is your own Higher Self, Inner Self, or Divine Self. This is the essence of who you really are, separate from your ego. Consciously invoking this presence brings a level of support that is in your highest good, separate from what your mind or ego thinks is best.

Flower Essence Support

If you have difficulty connecting with your Higher Self or GodSelf, you might want to consider using *A Way to the GodSelf Formula*™ flower essence.

Saguaro Cactus flower essence helps us to access and trust our inner wisdom.

Even if you are not sure that you have a Higher Self or GodSelf, you might want to experiment and include this presence anyway. You will be able to tell if it makes a difference when you contemplate what happens when this presence is included.

Other People

It is possible to have the essential support of any kind of teacher, guru, spiritual master, special family member, etc., whether they are alive or not. We can consciously invoke their spiritual presence for support if we want to.

Think about the people who have influenced your life in a powerful way. Who has been pivotal in helping you? Some of us may have studied different healing modalities that made a profound difference in our lives. You may want to call upon those teachers.

Was there a family member who provided a special kind of emotional support and whom you feel particularly good about? One client told me about her "cookie person". This woman was an older cousin who always provided a softening and supportive influence when she was growing up. When this cousin would arrive for a visit, she always brought chocolate chip cookies and an open ear for listening to my client's woes. When my client decided to invoke her healing support team, she immediately wanted to include her cousin.

There may be other people you would like to include who have provided a great spiritual support to you: a minister, priest, or a spiritual counselor of any sort. Friends may also be included as part of your healing support team. At any time you can call upon the Higher Self of another person to be part of your healing team.

For some of us it is a challenge to accept support from others. Many of us have been taught that it is better to give than to receive. However, it is important to have balance in our lives and receiving allows others the opportunity to give. The willingness to receive is required for healing to take place.

Flower Essence Support

If you have difficulty receiving support, you might want to consider using the *Giving & Receiving Support Formula*™ to create harmony with this issue.

The Angelic Realm

There is a great realm of angelic support available to us, whether or not we are conscious of it. You might want to invoke members of the angelic realm, such as your guardian angel; the angels of healing, including the Archangel Raphael; and any others with whom you feel an affinity.

There is an angelic presence for every aspect of life we experience. If you are having a specific challenge with an aspect of your life, let's say in a relationship, you might want to invoke the angel of harmonious relationships and the angel of the particular relationship with which you are having difficulty.

You can invoke the angel of any group or community. For instance, if you are experiencing difficulty with a family member, you can invoke the angel of your family and the particular family member's guardian angel.

In a business relationship you can invoke the angel of the specific business. Or you can invoke the angel of that type of business. If you need support in a printing matter, you can invoke the angel that presides over the function of printing. For more information about the angelic realm, see Dorothy Maclean's wonderful book, *To Hear the Angels Sing*.[1]

By invoking the angelic realm, you are inviting the consciousness behind the situation, event, relationship, etc., to bring you information and inspiration. To begin working with the angelic realm, you need simply to take the time to develop a relationship with this other form of consciousness. Any good relationship takes time to develop. If we cultivate a relationship with the angelic realm, we will build a strong foundation for our healing support team, from which we can draw powerful and timely help.

Flower Essence Support

If you want to enhance your relationship with the angelic realm, you might want to use the *Deepening Inner Union Formula*™.

Qualities

An essential part of our healing support team is the invocation of qualities. What is a quality? It is a focused and harmonious energetic state of fineness or excellence. When we experience discomfort, unease, or disharmony, we can invoke the quality that will help us transmute it into a state of harmony.

Recently I heard a song in two-part harmony. It had a most soothing effect and I felt as if my soul was being fed. The words to the song were not special or even interesting, but the sound of the two voices blending in harmony felt sublime.

---

1   *To Hear the Angels Sing*, Dorothy Maclean, Lorian Press, 1980.

The dictionary defines *harmony* as the *consistent, orderly or pleasing arrangement of parts*, and that it is *agreement or accord*. There are many parts or aspects of ourselves: our inner father, inner mother, inner child, inner masculine, and our inner feminine to name just a few. Our emotions, thoughts, spiritual self, intuition, and convictions are a few other aspects of ourselves.

When we have the experience that all (or most) of these parts are getting along harmoniously, we feel able, capable, and at peace with ourselves. When we haven't recognized or honored each of these inner aspects, we may live in a state of disharmony without even realizing it. We may feel out of sorts or vaguely unhappy with something about our lives. Until we fully honor ourselves we may not experience harmony.

Flower essences help us to see, understand, and honor the different parts of ourselves. They bring us into this state of harmony effortlessly. One person recently told me, "I am very impressed with your flower essences. Especially when in a crisis or intense situation, the calmness and clarity that I experience by using desert flower essences is awesome." Calmness and clarity are two of the side effects of the effortless harmony created by flower essences.

I have found that harmony is an extremely important step in the process of healing and evolving in consciousness. When we make harmony the focal point of our healing journey, we can have great success. One of the laws of the universe is that what we focus on expands. When we focus on disharmony and symptoms, they grow more menacing and difficult. Yet once we recognize the disharmony, we can consciously look for the quality, or qualities, that can relieve it. When we invoke, or call forth, those qualities, we find them in the midst of our pain.

Once we begin to focus on the qualities that we want to experience, we find that it becomes easier to accept the apparent disharmony as an opportunity. Our perspective begins to change and the challenges that once stopped us, or kept us in pain, become the stepping stones to a fuller experience of harmony.

Following is a sample list of qualities that I like to invoke. Select the qualities that appeal to you, ones that you particularly want to enhance in your life. As you contemplate this list you may discover favorite qualities of your own that you want to add to it. You may find that this list will become an important place to turn when you are not sure of what you need. It can provide inspiration and support as you take responsibility for your inner state, and you recognize what you want to create within yourself.

- clarity
- focus
- love
- healing
- wisdom
- deliverance
- joy
- playfulness
- humility
- compassion
- understanding
- integrity
- tenderness
- creativity
- mercy
- kindness
- goodness
- benevolence
- holiness
- full self-expression
- purity

- warmth
- balance
- sacredness
- blessedness
- peace
- harmony
- generosity
- abundance
- gentleness
- selflessness
- harmlessness
- calmness
- centeredness
- groundedness
- unity with God or the Creator
- bliss
- gratitude
- enthusiasm
- patience
- humor
- delight

Don't forget that you can add qualities and other support members to your healing support team as you go along. When I was first inspired to create a healing support team, there were a few important members and qualities. As the years went by, more members and qualities have been added so that it is now a large and inclusive support team.

Flower Essence Support

If you have difficulty being clear about the qualities you want to include in your healing support team, you can use *Claret Cup Hedgehog Cactus* flower essence for support in finding clarity.

Exercise: Creating Your Healing Support Team

Take a few moments to do the following contemplation exercise. Be sure that you have a quiet and uninterrupted space in which to focus on the following three questions. Contemplation means to be in the temple of our own inner wisdom. As you do this exercise, allow yourself to go within your own inner temple where clarity and answers reside.

Take a minute to quiet yourself and focus on receiving three deep breaths. When you feel ready, ask yourself the following questions:

1. Who on the earth has been a supportive teacher whose wisdom could possibly help me? Would I like them to be part of my healing support team?

☘ A meditation teacher or guru

☘ A therapist

❀ A teacher of a particular healing modality

❀ A special friend

❀ A trusted family member

Invoke their spiritual presence to be part of your healing support team by simply asking. It is best to speak the invocation out loud as it is a manifestation of your intent:

> "I now invite (or invoke) _____
> to be a part of my healing support team."

2. Which members of the formless realm would you like to have supporting you?

❀ The devas and nature spirits of the desert (or other geographical area)

❀ Members of the angelic realm (the Archangel Raphael, the angel of a relationship, etc.)

❀ A trusted departed family member

❀ A great teacher from ages past (Gautama Buddha, Jesus, Krishna, Mohammed, Paracelcus, Socrates, etc.)

Invoke their spiritual presence to be part of your healing support team by simply asking.

3. Invoke the qualities you would like to support you. You can use the list on page 59 as a guide, or add any others that you want. Invoke these qualities to be part of your healing support team by simply asking for them.

4. Empower your group to work together as a team by asking that you all work together for the good of the whole earth, specifically through your personal healing and evolution.

Once you have invoked your healing support team, you can invoke the group in the future by simply saying, "I invoke my healing support team to be with me now." Don't forget that you may want to add additional members or qualities to the team to deal with specific issues.

———

Chapter 7

STEP TWO:
DEFINING YOUR INTENTION

Without knowing where you want to go,
how can you get there?

BEFORE WE SELECT FLOWER essences it is important to know what it is that we want them to address. What kind of support do we want? What is it that is pushing us to seek the aid of flower essences? The clearer we are, the more accurate we will be in finding the flower essences that will help us make a desired change. To do this we need to define our intention.

What is intention, and why is it important in selecting flower essences? Intention is the act in which we determine the result we want to achieve. When we define our intention, we create a specific focal point for selecting flower essences. By deciding what we want to change or harmonize, we can effectively choose the precise flower essences that will help us make these changes. By defining our intention for using the flower essences, we can empower ourselves to select the ones that will help in harmonizing the core or root of a situation with which we feel discomfort.

Many of us have been taught that, when it comes to healing, we are powerless. This is not true. When we consciously decide to take responsibility for our own healing process, we find the healing tools and facilitators that can help us.

We can always attempt to see what role we have played in creating any health issue. Flower essences are perfect for helping us become more conscious of the emotional, attitudinal, and spiritual significance behind any healing project. We attract the healing support we need by consciously defining our intention.

The few moments we spend being clear about our intention could well be the most important part of selecting flower essences. No matter what method you use for selecting flower essences, whether it is intuitive or a more linear approach, you will receive high quality support if you first define your purpose by clarifying what you want the essences to address.

Part One: Identify Your Needs

For many people the greatest challenge in selecting flower essences is in being clear about what they want the flower essences to address. "There's so much I want to change," they say. "Where do I start? What is the most important thing to work with first? Will I choose the 'right' thing to work with?"

Everything in our lives is related. All the discomforts we experience are indicators of underlying issues that want resolution. The things that seem unrelated are usually all linked to a common underlying disharmony. The seemingly unimportant discomforts we experience are linked with our most challenging issues through the underlying cause.

Many of us have to overcome the tendency to think that there is a perfect, or right, thing to work with. Because we don't know what this thing is, we feel helpless to begin. Whatever is in front of us right now is the place to start. If we have an issue with a certain relationship today, we can begin with that. It will be linked to the most important underlying issue. If we simply begin with what is right in front of us now, we will have success.

After you have done the first step and invoked healing support, attune to your inner Self. Invite yourself to go within, to be clear about why you want the support of flower essences at this time. Why do you want to select a flower essence for yourself right now? Are you feeling discomfort with an issue, a person, with yourself? You might ask yourself one or more of the following questions:

- ❀ What is going on within myself?

- ❀ What discomfort am I feeling?

- ❀ What sort of support do I want?

- ❀ What is it that I want to change in someone else? How might this be a reflection of something within myself?

- ❀ What do I want to change within myself?

- ❀ What is happening in my life that is pushing me to seek the aid of the flower essences?

- ❀ How do I want to be different?

- ❀ What am I feeling?

- ❀ What is my interpretation of this situation/feeling/person, etc.?

- ❀ How do I want to feel, as opposed to how I am feeling at this moment?

- ❀ In what area do I want the essences to help me?

Be as specific as possible. The more specific you are the more directly you will be able to address the root of your discomfort. If, in this process of identifying what is happening within yourself, you notice that you are belittling yourself, or judging yourself for the way you are feeling, you might want to include this as part of what you want the flower essences to address. This is a great starting place, the issue of self-love or self-acceptance.

Write down, either in great detail or in a short statement, what it is you want to work with in yourself. You may want to talk with a trusted friend, a therapist, write in your journal, or use *The Flower Essence Journal* in Appendix A to help you be clear about your needs. If you still cannot define what it is that you want to work with, there are two things you can do. One is that you can use the flower essence called the *Emotional Awareness Formula*™ to help you recognize and understand what is going on within yourself. Or, you can select flower essences to support you in having clarity. Use this as your intention and then select the flower essences that will support you to be clear.

If this process of defining your intention seems too daunting and you are unsure of what you want to work with, you might set your intention to find the most beneficial flower essences that will support your highest good at this time. Then, go on to the next part and select one or more qualities you would like to enhance within yourself. This is a very powerful and comprehensive intention, and you will be supported with everything you need.

EXAMPLE

Let's say that you are uncomfortable because your mother-in-law is coming to stay at your house and you usually feel belittled by her. You recognize that she is a challenging personality for you to deal with and, although you want her to visit, you are afraid that you will continually feel put down. You have defined the issue as being your emotional response to your mother-in-law and the feelings of unworthiness and incapability that you feel around her.

Part Two: Find the Harmonizing Qualities

Once you are clear about the disharmony or issue with which you want support, it is important to identify the qualities that will bring resolution. If you are having trouble with a particular disharmony, find its harmonizing quality. Of all the aspects of defining your intention, this is an essential element to understand and use.

For instance, if you have recognized that you are jealous and you want to change, you might want to select the harmonizing quality of compassion. Love can create harmony in situations of hate. If you are very disappointed about something, you can ask for support in feeling content with the situation.

You can explore the list of qualities on page 59 and search for one or more qualities that will harmonize the issue with which you want to work. If you are still not sure of which quality you need, select one or more that simply feel good to you and that you would like to enhance. Remember, what you focus on expands. If you focus on what promotes harmony, you will move more quickly out of your discomfort.

EXAMPLE

To take the previous example further, you might recognize that the qualities you want to experience when you are around your mother-in-law are *strength, self-empowerment,* and *capability.*

Part Three: Write Down Your Intention

Using the issue(s) that you identified in Part One, and the harmonizing qualities you selected in Part Two, write down a simple statement of what you want the flower essences to address. State the support you want in terms of the qualities you want to attain or strengthen within yourself.

It is helpful to formulate a statement that you can use as a foundation each time you want to select flower essences. In constructing this statement there are a few important things to consider. One is being clear about how deeply you want the essences to work. Do you want to address the core, or do you want to work superficially?

Another thing to consider is the time element. The type of support you seek is for what time? If we do not mention a time, we may find ourselves having selected the most beneficial flower essences we could have used a year ago for a particular issue. The more specific we are, the more specific the support will be for selecting flower essences to address exactly what we want.

Once you make a statement you might want to attempt to poke some holes in it as a way of testing its clarity. For instance, if your statement is, "I want to find the best flower essences for my depression," you might see that there are a lot of misunderstandings that can result. "Best" is in relation to what? Are you asking to find flower essences that will help you to feel depressed? Are you asking for flower essences that would have helped you a year ago when you were depressed?

Even if it seems silly or picky to analyze your statement, it is always supportive to be as clear as possible. You will find that you will get what you ask for. The result will not be all you hoped for if you are not clear when you make your intention statement.

Following are samples of some intention statements that you could use by filling in the blanks. Alternatively, you can adapt them with your own creativity.

- ❀ *My intention is to select the most beneficial flower essence(s) to support my highest good at this time in enhancing (qualities) _____ , so I can experience harmony with the core cause of (name the issue or concern with which you want to work) _____ .*

- ❀ *I want to select flower essences that will help me to experience (qualities) _____ , so I can fully heal at this time (issue with which you want to work) _____ .*

- ❀ *I want to select the most beneficial flower essences for my highest good at this time to feel (qualities) _____ .*

- ❀ *My intention is to select the most beneficial flower essences for my highest good at this time as I feel (qualities) _____ and harmonize (issue) _____ .*

Once you have defined your intention statement, use it as an anchoring point before you select flower essences. You can use this same statement whether you use a pendulum, kinesiology, the flower cards, a cross-reference, or any other method for selecting flower essences. It provides a clear and concise foundation for any selection method. You can use this statement when you are selecting flower essences for yourself or for others.

EXAMPLE

To continue with our mother-in-law example, you might write the following statement: "I want to find the most beneficial flower essences for my highest good at this time in being strong, self-empowered, and capable, so that I can heal the core of the disharmony I feel in my mother-in-law's presence."

If you have difficulty defining your intention, consider the goal of having clarity about your inner state and needs. You may want to select and use flower essences to support you with identifying your inner needs and expressing them in a few short sentences. Alternatively, you might consider using the *Emotional Awareness Formula™* to promote clarity about your inner state.

Flower Essence Support

When faced with the difficulty of defining the support you want to have from the flower essences, you might use the *Emotional Awareness Formula™* to help you be aware of your inner state, thus helping you know what you need.

Chapter 8

—

STEP THREE:
SELECTING THE FLOWER ESSENCES

The process of selecting flower essences can be
an exciting journey in learning more about yourself.

ONCE YOU HAVE INVOKED your healing support team and defined your intention, there are many different methods for selecting the flower essences. Many people like to use a pendulum. This is the method I use, and I find it simple and accurate.
Perhaps one of the simplest methods is using flower cards. There
are several ways to use flower cards, all of which are easy and
fun. Many folks like using a cross-reference where they can look
up a desired state of being and find the flower essences to help.
Intuitive impression is another method. Others find that kinesiology works best for them.

It is fine to use the method that is most comfortable for you.
Not every person will take to using a pendulum. For some, kinesiology may seem difficult. What is most important is that
you use a method for selecting flower essences that feels good
and with which you ultimately develop confidence. Any method

may seem a little awkward at first. Riding a bicycle for the first few times was probably a challenge as well.

Whatever method you use to select flower essences can lead you to trusting your intuition because you will be able to evaluate the effects of using the essences you selected. You will be your own scientific laboratory, observing the effects of the flower essences you chose.

All of the above methods will be discussed in this chapter. As you master one or more of the methods, you will soon cultivate a deeper relationship with your intuition.

When you select flower essences it is good to have a set of essences to use for most of the methods of selecting. Many folks like to own a complete set of flower essences. If you have a partial set, don't worry. You can start with what you have and slowly build up. So many of us worry that what we need is "out there". What we need is usually right in front of us, or it comes easily into our lives. Even with a small set of flower essences you can create great support for yourself.

If you do not have a set of flower essences, you can use flower cards to select them. There have been many people over the years who have excitedly approached me after a presentation in which I have shown slides of the flowers. They ask me about a particular flower, telling me that they have seen it in their dreams or meditation. When they discover that it is a flower from which an essence is made, they invariably find that the essence is a perfect fit for resolving an important issue.

When you ask for support, and open yourself to receive it, nature will find you in a way that is unique to you and your needs.

How Many Essences to Use

Combining flower essences is an art. When we make an art-ful blend, the essences will work together synergistically. How many essences can we use together at one time? The most common number of essences that I usually combine is between three and five. Occasionally more than that will be indicated, but it is rare. However, when I first began selecting flower essences, it was common for me to select as many as eight or nine. There are also many times when I use just one.

In our seminars where we teach the methods for selecting the essences, it is common for folks to choose a greater number at first. If this happens, don't worry. You might want to review the intention that you defined and check it for clarity. The clearer your intention, the more precise your essence selection will be.

That said, don't worry if you select a greater number of flower essences at first. Just use the essences and then evaluate their effects to learn about them, the process, and yourself. As your confidence in yourself increases, your trust in the process will also increase.

The following sections will include detailed instructions for using five different methods to select flower essences. You will probably find that one of these methods will feel more natural to you than the others. The process of selecting flower essences can be an exciting journey in learning more about yourself and going beyond your self-imposed limitations. May your journey be a delightful one!

❀ Using a Pendulum

❀ Using Intuitive Impression

❀ Using Flower Cards

❀ Using Kinesiology

❀ Using a Cross-reference

Using a Pendulum

A pendulum is a simple tool for indicating our intuitive wisdom. It is not always the quickest method to learn, but once you have mastered it you will have learned to trust yourself and your intuition, which is a huge benefit for using this method. Learning to use a pendulum can take five minutes or five months, depending on your relationship with your intuition. If you want to learn to recognize and trust your intuition, this method could be for you.

In the past few years I have heard and read a lot of very strange things about using pendulums. There are folks who teach that a pendulum is an entity that can solve all your problems and know what is best for you. If you want to use a pendulum for those purposes, this chapter is not for you.

When I first began to use a pendulum, I had no real instruction. I made important discoveries about using a pendulum by doing some really foolish things with it. Once I started experimenting with my pendulum, I excitedly used it to select all sorts of things: which clothes to buy; which people might be best to have in my life; whether I should do this or that; and lots of other nonsensical things. I went completely overboard with it, empowering my pendulum to have all the answers to my important questions of life.

One day I used my pendulum in a department store to select which bed sheets would be most beneficial for me to buy. The pendulum indicated some sheets that I really didn't like, but I bought them anyway, because my pendulum knew best.

This experience was a blessing because it showed me how I had empowered my pendulum with having wisdom. Having to live with ugly bed sheets showed me how ignorant I had been in using the pendulum. I threw the pendulum away and stopped using it for several months.

This experience helped me to realize the real function of a pendulum. It is a tool that indicates your own inner wisdom. If you understand nothing else from this chapter, I hope you really hear this: a pendulum is not an entity.

A pendulum is not an entity. It will not tell you anything. It cannot decide things for you. It is not a higher power that can solve all of your life issues. It is like a screwdriver. It is simply a tool that we use to indicate what our intuition knows. A pendulum does not have power. The power is within ourselves and is in harmony with the healing and angelic support we have invoked.

When used properly, a pendulum will be an outer indicator of your own inner wisdom. Once I became experienced with using a pendulum, I discovered that I could select flower essences without it, running my hand over the flower essences and sensing which ones were appropriate. However, I have to focus with more concentration to be as accurate as when I use a pendulum. Today I continue to use a pendulum as my main method for selecting flower essences because it is a very convenient tool.

For years I did not want to share about how to use a pendulum because I was concerned that folks would do as I did and empower a pendulum with wisdom and expect it to give them answers. I am still amazed, when in workshops I make a big point about a pendulum not being an entity, that later folks tell me, "Oh, when I asked my pendulum if I should _____ it told me _____."

A pendulum cannot tell you anything. Your pendulum is a piece of metal, stone, or crystal and does not have the wisdom to give you answers. Please do not attempt to ask your pendulum to give you answers. It is important to be very clear that the answers come from your own wisdom and that the pendulum is just a tool for helping you to recognize them.

The most important things that we develop when we use a pendulum are self-trust and acceptance of our intuition. As you learn to use a pendulum as a tool, you will come face to face with any of your feelings of self-doubt, distrust of your intuition, and inadequacy. You will probably wonder if you are doing it right. You will likely question if you are making the pendulum indicate the response you want. It's all right to have questions and concerns. They are a natural part of the process of learning.

As you practice using a pendulum you will learn to listen to your intuition, to trust it, and to see when your mind is too involved. After you select flower essences intuitively with a pendulum, you will be able to engage your rational mind by studying the essences you have selected. With careful documentation of your process, you will be able to evaluate if, and how, the essences were appropriate for the intention you set up. As you watch yourself in the process of selecting and using the flower essences, you will learn to trust yourself, and you will gain confidence in working with your intuition.

What Kind of Pendulum to Use

There are many different pendulums available on the market today. They can be found made of crystal, wood, metal, or stone. Some are made from semi-precious stones, glass, or carved wooden beads.

When you select a pendulum, it is important that it feels good to you. I have found that the pendulums that move the easiest have a more or less traditional pendulum shape (see figure 2 on page 78). They should be light enough to move easily but heavy enough to keep it from swinging wildly. Your pendulum should not be so heavy that your fingers tire easily. Selecting a pendulum is a personal thing, and it is important to try them out by swinging them and seeing how they feel.

Pendulums range in price from $4 to $400 depending on the materials used. It is beneficial to keep your pendulum in a little pouch for safekeeping. These are usually available wherever quality pendulums are sold.

The length of the string or chain is a matter of personal preference. You want to be able to hold the chain of your pendulum comfortably between your index finger and thumb (see figure 3 on page 79). It can be very grounding to have the end of the chain, which usually has a stone or metal bead, anchored in your palm. The pendulum itself should swing freely at the other end of the chain. The chain should be flexible enough to allow easy movement.

If the chain is too long, the pendulum will be slow to start and may not move easily. If the chain is too short, the pendulum may swing too fast and hit your fingers or hand. I like to have about two and a half inches of chain from the top of the pendulum to where I hold it be-

Fig. 2

tween my fingers. I like to anchor the other end of the chain
in the palm of my hand, so there
needs to be enough chain to
reach.

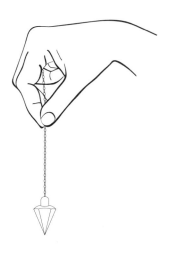

You can make your own
pendulum if you want. You can
use a necklace chain, some sort
of thread, or even dental floss,
for the chain. For the pendulum
weight you can use a pendant, a
ring, or any other light-weighted
object that can be suspended
from a string or chain. However,
pendulums that are made from
objects that do not have a pendulum shape usually will not
swing as fluidly.

FIG. 3

The Mechanics of Using a Pendulum

A pendulum is an outer tool that indicates our own intuitive wisdom. When we use it properly, it indicates by a recognizable movement something that we know with our intuition.
To use a pendulum, we must first establish a language. We need
to set up a consistently recognizable movement for our pendulum to indicate affirmative and negative responses.

Many folks use a clockwise direction to indicate an affirmative response and an anti-clockwise movement to indicate a negative response. Others may use a forward-backwards movement
to indicate an affirmative response and a left-right movement

for the negative indicator. The direction you use is not important. What is important is that, once you establish the communication system, you honor it and use it consistently.

Exercise: Establishing your Pendulum Language

For this exercise you will need a pendulum. Hold your pendulum in your hand, with the chain between your index finger and thumb. Rest the end of the pendulum chain in the palm of your hand, gently holding the end bead against your palm with your little, ring, and middle fingers.

Feel the weight of your pendulum. The first time you held a screwdriver or other tool it probably felt a little strange to you. Spend some time becoming familiar with this simple tool's movements and how it feels in your hand.

Some people think that their arm is not supposed to move the pendulum. They hold their arm stiff, strangling any natural movement their arm wants to make, and stare pointedly at their pendulum, waiting for it to move of its own accord. Since a pendulum is not an entity, it will not move of its own accord. Allow your arm to relax. Hold your pendulum firmly but gently, and allow your arm to move it.

Play with moving your pendulum clockwise, anti-clockwise, forward and backward, left and right. Get a feel for how this tool moves. Which directions are most comfortable? Which movements feel natural to you?

Once you feel comfortable with the different movements, decide which movement you want to indicate an affirmative answer. Practice by moving your pendulum in this direction. Get the feel of it. Practice until it feels natural for you. You now have established the language for an affirmative answer.

Then, decide which direction you want to indicate a negative response. Practice by moving your pendulum in that direction until it feels very comfortable. You have now established the language for a negative response.

Once you are comfortable with your affirmative and negative response movements, you will have your communication system set up. Write down these movements below so that you don't forget them in the future.

Answers of "Yes"
are indicated by the
following movement: _____

Answers of "No"
are indicated by the
following movement: _____

Occasionally you might not get a clear "yes" or "no" response when you test for a flower essence. Sometimes your pendulum might move in an unclear way or a different direction from the ones above. If you get an unclear response it probably means that your statement needs clarity or it is dubious. If this happens, go back and look at your intention statement. See if you can be more precise. Sometimes an unclear movement can indicate a "neutral" response, and your question or statement does not have a clear "yes" or "no" answer. It may also indicate that you are not focusing on your statement, that you might be distracted and not really paying attention to what you are doing.

The more you use your pendulum the more confident you will become. Remember: a pendulum is a tool and the way to master any tool is through practice. You will have doubts when you first use a pendulum. This is natural. You will wonder if your are doing it right. This is all right. The process will teach you a lot about yourself, your intuition, and your self-confidence.

Selecting Flower Essences with a Pendulum

When we use a pendulum to select flower essences it is helpful, but not necessary, to have the essences in a kit box or some other container. It is natural for your mind to want to be involved in the process of selecting the essences and, indeed, your mind will play an important role. However, while you use your pendulum you can invite your rational mind to take a back seat and reassure it that it will have its turn shortly. Listen to what your mind says as you go through the process of selecting the flower essences, but don't let it dominate the process. This is an intuitive method for selecting flower essences, and it's your intuition's turn when you use your pendulum.

If your flower essences are in a box or container, turn the bottles so that their labels are facing away from you and you cannot see the names of the essences. This will help you to be impartial and not engage your mind at this point. If your flower essences are not in a box or container, arrange them randomly and so that you cannot see the names.

Step 1: Invocation

Invoke your healing support team. (See Chapter 6.)

Step 2: Intention

Clarify your intention for using flower essences at this time. (See Chapter 7.)

Step 3: Select the Flower Essences

Select the flower essences that resonate with the intention you created. Lay your hand over one box of flower essences. With your pendulum held comfortably in your other hand, give it a little swing to get it started. Wait to see if you have an affirmative or negative response. If you have a negative response, put the first box aside and go on to the next box or container in the same way.

If you have an affirmative response, open the box and touch one bottle at a time, waiting to see if you have an affirmative or negative response. When you have an affirmative response, take the essence out of the box and set it aside. Go on to check all of the other essences in the same way. If your essences are not in a box or container touch each essence, one at a time, in the same way as above. Set aside any essences that have been indicated.

Once you have gone through all of the essences, write down the names of the ones you have selected. Then, engage your rational mind and study each essence to see if, and how, it applies to you. It is helpful to look up the harmonizing qualities and patterns of imbalance with which each essence works.[1] Write down which patterns you recognize in yourself and which qualities you most want to enhance within yourself. Keep an open mind as you study the flower essence as there is usually a reason for the essence's appearance, even if you don't consciously understand it immediately. If you don't see the essence's relevancy, write this down as well.

Be aware that the patterns and qualities are only a guide. Not all the patterns of imbalance may apply to you. You don't need to embrace them as your own unless you recognize them within yourself. If you don't recognize any of the listed pat-

---

1   You can refer to *The Alchemy of the Desert* for
patterns and qualities of desert flower essences
or visit the web site at *www.desert-alchemy.com*.

terns, keep an open mind. As you use the essence, see if you recognize any of the patterns acting within you. You might want to read about each essence from time to time as you use them. This will help you contemplate events, feelings and situations in your life and see how any of the harmonizing qualities of the flower essence, or its patterns of imbalance, are at work within you.

Step 4: Use the Flower Essences

See Chapter 9 for information about using the flower essences.

Step 5: Evaluate the Effects

After you have finished using the flower essences, take time to evaluate the effects. This will give you the chance to see for yourself what effects or changes have occurred. Evaluating the effects of using the flower essences is an important part of building confidence with selecting flower essences intuitively. (See Chapter 10.)

...I remembered you saying that at one time you used to select flower essences each morning to support you through you day. After completing your class, I timidly started to select flower essences each day using a pendulum. At first it took me about forty-five minutes to complete the steps, and I must say that I doubted my selections. But the process of going through invocation and then defining my intention helped me to have confidence. Even more, every evening when I would sit down and evaluate how the essences might have supported me that day, I found that my selections were really perfect. This gave me even more confidence to continue using my pendulum.

Now, it is six months after I began selecting flower essences for myself and I find that it takes me only about ten minutes in the morning to go through the steps and select the flower essences for my day. My self-confidence has really increased. I find that it is easier to trust my intuition, which as always been a big challenge for me. Your method for selecting flower essences has helped me as much as the essences themselves.

~ J. T., Arizona

Challenges & Solutions

Once you select flower essences in this way, it is not helpful to re-test the same flower essences again. It is more supportive to follow through and use the essences indicated and then evaluate their effects. If we attempt to re-test the essences, we are giving our intuitive-self a message of distrust. We inspire confidence by honoring and following through.

If we use flower essences that we do not need, nothing will happen, so it is safe to use yourself as a testing ground. When we select flower essences that we do need, there will be either subtle or prominent effects that we will probably be able to recognize. If you feel you are having difficulty in evaluating the effects, you can work with a trusted friend or with a professional flower essence practitioner until you gain more confidence. Even folks who are very experienced in selecting flower essences for themselves sometimes need outside support for working with specific issues.

If you experience challenges with the process of using a pendulum, you might want to select flower essences to help you with the challenge you are experiencing. For instance, if you find that you are judging and criticizing yourself, you might want to select flower essences to help harmonize this tendency. Alternatively, you can use one or more of the following flower essences to help you with the process of selecting flower essences with a pendulum:

Flower Essence Support

Desert Christmas Cholla Cactus used together with *Making & Honoring Boundaries Formula*™ provides a general support for the process of learning to use a pendulum.

Foothills Paloverde – To harmonize self-judgement, allowing your mind to take a back seat and not dominate the process.

Queen of the Night Cactus supports you in honoring your intuition.

Indian Root – For the tendency to make things hard and difficult, especially if you think it can't be so simple.

Using Intuitive Impression

Intuitive impression is a phrase I use to describe a direct intuitive sensing of the flower essences that are appropriate to use. Intuitive impression is probably the most challenging of the different intuitive methods to use for selecting flower essences. However, for those who have a developed intuitive sense, it can be the easiest.

Many people who become proficient at using an intuitive method for selecting flower essences, such as a pendulum, flower cards, or kinesiology, may find that they spontaneously experience intuitive impression on occasion. It seems that by practicing the intuitive method, they have exercised their "intuitive muscle", which has become a more integrated part of them.

There are different ways in which we can experience intuitive impression. Basically it is a sensing of the image or name of the flower essence(s) that are in alignment with the intention we defined in Step Two of the Five-Step Process. We may "see", "hear", "smell" or "sense" a particular flower that corresponds to a need that we have. I have experienced intuitive impression in these different ways.

Sometimes I "see" the name of the flower or an image of the flower itself. This is an inner sensing and not a seeing with my physical eyes. Often this happens when someone is describing a state of being with which she is having a difficult time. I will "see" the image of a flower. It is often not the flower essence I would have chosen with my mind, but it is always a flower essence that has deep meaning and support for the person.

On many occasions when I have given public presentations that include slide shows of the flowers, one or more persons will approach me afterwards and ask about a particular flower. He or she will invariably tell me that they have seen that flower either in meditation, in a dream, or in a waking state and that they want to know its name. When I tell them the name of the flower and they read about its qualities, they tell me that it is exactly what they need at that time to help them with a particular issue. This is one way in which intuitive impression works with many people.

"Hearing" the name of a flower is another way in which intuitive impression may manifest. Very often when someone is talking to me about a particular issue I "hear" the name of a certain flower essence. As they speak, it is as if the flower is also speaking its name to me at the same time.

Another way in which we experience intuitive impression is when we "feel" something when we touch a flower essence that corresponds with the intention we have defined. We may sense a tingling sensation in our fingers or a sensation of heat or coolness. This sensation only happens with the flower essences that are in alignment with our intention.

There have been a few times when I will "smell" a particular flower when someone is talking about an issue with which they want resolution. Once again, this is an "inner" smelling and not something that anyone else seems to smell. It is a way in which a flower is calling, or reaching out, to be noticed, and it invariably leads to a flower essence that provides a great support for the person.

Probably the most important thing about intuitive impression is that there is not any "doing" involved. As a matter of fact, the more you try the further you will be from having this experience. To master intuitive impression you need to just let go and allow your intuition to bring this experience to you. You might experience the "sensing" or the "hearing" type of intuitive impression. Or, it might come to you through an inner "seeing".

You can experiment with intuitive impression. Be willing to let go of all concepts about how it will happen for you. I think that intuitive impression is the simplest way to intuitively select flower essences, but it requires the most focus and the highest degree of letting go and receptivity.

How to Use Intuitive Impression

Step 1: Invocation

Invoke your healing support team. (See Chapter 6.)

Step 2: Intention

Define your intention. (See Chapter 7.)

Step 3: Select the Flower Essences

Invite yourself to be open and receptive to the intelligence of nature. If you do not receive an impression, or "hear" the name of a flower essence, or "see" a particular image of a flower, touch each of the bottles of flower essences with your eyes closed. Allow yourself to sense which of the essences are in alignment with your intention. See if you can tell a difference between the essences as you touch them. Write down the names of any essences you have selected. Then, look up their descriptions and see if any of the patterns of imbalance or harmonizing qualities apply. Write these down. If none of them seem to apply, write this down as well.

Step 4: Use the Flower Essences

See Chapter 9 for information about using the flower essences.

Step 5: Evaluation

It's important to follow up and see what you have experienced after using the flower essences. This will help to more fully develop trust in the process of selecting flower essences with intuitive impression, as well as give yourself the opportunity to see what effects you may have experienced with the use of the flower essences. See Chapter 10 for information about how to evaluate the effects.

Using Flower Cards

A feast for the eyes and the soul

Flower cards are a wonderful way to work with flower essences through visual attunement. This is probably the simplest method for selecting flower essences. Because it is so easy to select flower essences this way, some people at first think it couldn't really work. However, the feedback we receive from folks shows that they have tremendous success by using flower cards. The flower cards can make flower essence selection available to teens, children, busy folks, and anyone wishing to have a simple method for selecting the essences.

Flower essences can make a huge difference in teenagers' attitudes and give them better understanding of the deep changes taking place within them. By using the flower cards, they can select flower essences and begin to take more responsibility for themselves.

Children have a great inner wisdom about what is right for them. By using the flower cards, they can utilize and honor this wisdom easily and effectively.

Many men, who had said in the past that they couldn't relate to the concept of the flower essences, found that seeing a picture of the flower made flower essences more real to them.

Experienced flower essence practitioners and self-help users found that seeing the flower expanded their attunement and understanding of the flower essence. The shape, color and form of a flower speaks to our soul, our mind and our heart, bringing another dimension to our experience of the essences.

Invoking your healing support team and defining your intention is vital for creating the foundation for selecting the flower essences that you really want as you use the flower cards. Following are four different methods for using flower cards. You can also create your own method if you are inspired.

The Attraction/Aversion Method

This is an easy and fun method for selecting flower essences for which we have had impressive feedback. It is so simple that many people at first think it is too easy. However, once they look up the descriptions of the flowers they have chosen, they are usually impressed with the results.

Step 1: Invocation

Invoke your healing support team. (See Chapter 6.)

Step 2: Intention

Define your intention. (See Chapter 7.)

Step 3: Select the Flower Essences

Go through the deck, card by card, and notice which images particularly attract you. Set these cards aside. Also notice which cards repulse you or with which you have a response of dislike. Set these cards aside with the other ones. If there are more than five cards, go through the cards you have set aside and select up to five cards for which you have a strong like or dislike. Look up the descriptions of the flower essences and write down any of the patterns of imbalance and harmonizing qualities that you feel apply to you.

Step 4: Use the Flower Essences

Use the corresponding flower essences. (See Chapter 9.) Keep the cards in a readily visible place while you are using them.

Step 5: Evaluation

Evaluate the effects of the flower essences when you have finished using them. (See Chapter 10.)

The flower cards have opened a whole new opportunity for my fifteen-year-old daughter and her friends. She used to say, 'Oh, Mom!' when I would select flower essences for her.

I brought home your flower cards and suggested that she select flower essences herself. The first time she selected three cards that she really liked and one that she really disliked [using the attraction/aversion method]. She used the corresponding flower essences and I am amazed at the change in her.

She used to be extremely shy and had little self-confidence. Since using the flower essences she selected, she tried out for a role in the drama club and seems really happy about it. I am amazed.

But best of all, now she and her girlfriends use the cards and the essences on a regular basis. It is so heartwarming to see the changes in them and their eagerness to use flower essences now. Thank you for providing an easy way for selecting flower essences!

~ D. S., California

Flower Card Draw

Step 1: Invocation

Invoke your healing support team. (See Chapter 6.)

Step 2: Intention

Define your intention. (See Chapter 7.)

Step 3: Select the Flower Essences

Spread the cards out, face down, and draw up to five cards. Notice any impressions you have when you see the images of the flowers. Look up the descriptions of the flower essences and write down any of the patterns of imbalance and harmonizing qualities that you feel apply to you.

Step 4: Use the Flower Essences

Use the corresponding flower essences. (See Chapter 9.) Keep the cards in a readily visible place while you are using them.

Step 5: Evaluation

Evaluate the effects of the flower essences when you have finished using them. (See Chapter 10.)

My boyfriend has always been supportive of my using flower essences but it wasn't until I showed him the flower cards that he got interested in selecting and using any for himself. The changes in him are really big, and best of all, he can see them in himself! He has an uncanny ability to describe how the shape and form of the flower reminds him of aspects of himself. I am amazed.

~ L. H., Arizona

The Flower Power Circle

This is a very popular way to use the flower cards. A circle can define a sacred and protected space. This method makes trusting your intuition easy. Spread the cards out, facing down, in a large circle on the floor. Sit in the middle of the circle, surrounded by the cards

Step 1: Invocation

Invoke your healing support team. (See Chapter 6.)

Step 2: Intention

Define your intention. (See Chapter 7.)

Step 3: Select the Flower Essences

With your eyes closed, allow your hand to pass lightly over the cards around you. One or more cards will attract you. Some folks feel a warm or cool sensation when their hand passes over the appropriate card(s). Others simply sense which card or cards are appropriate. Even if you experience doubt while you are selecting a card, you will be able to verify your selection when you look up the descriptions of the flower essences you have chosen. It is wise to limit your selection to no more than five cards at one time. Look up the descriptions of the flower cards you have chosen. Write down the patterns of imbalance and harmonizing qualities with which you identify. If you don't recognize any of the patterns or qualities, write that down as well and keep an open mind.

Step 4: Use the Flower Essences

Use the corresponding flower essences. (See Chapter 9.) Keep the cards in a readily visible place while you are using them.

Step 5: Evaluation

Evaluate the effects of the flower essences when you have finished using them. (See Chapter 10.)

Last week I began feeling really needy of support. I called and tried to get a flower essence consultation session with you but there weren't any sessions available until next week. Out of desperation, I sat down, got out my notes from the workshop, and decided to just try using the flower cards following the way you taught us. My mind was very skeptical, but I went ahead anyway.

Using the flower power circle method I laid the cards out in a circle. I sat in the middle of the circle and invoked my healing group as you showed us. Then, I took time to become clear about what kind of support I wanted.

I ended up selecting four cards, and then I read each chapter in [The Alchemy of the Desert] book. I was astounded. They were so perfect! I felt so much support from the words in the book. It was like having a coaching session, but I didn't need to go anywhere. I went to the store and purchased the four indicated essences and have begun to use them.

It is now four days since I began using them and I have stopped feeling frantic and unsupported. I feel that I am capable of finding all the support I need to continue in this healing process I have begun. These flower essences have already helped by stopping my anxiety and are helping me to feel empowered in self-healing. ... Your system is incredibly simple, easy, and self-empowering. And best of all, I don't need to believe in anything. I can see how appropriate the essences are and it satisfies my skeptical mind. Thank you so much for your work.

~ K. M., California

Visual Attunement

If you are using a different method of selecting flower essences (such as a pendulum, kinesiology, or whatever) with which you are comfortable, the cards can be used as an additional aid to enhance your experience while using the essences.

Step 1: Invocation

Invoke your healing support team. (See Chapter 6.)

Step 2: Intention

Define your intention. (See Chapter 7.)

Step 3: Select the Flower Essences

Once you select the flower essences using your favorite method, find each corresponding card from the deck.

As you study each image of the flowers, allow yourself to attune to the flower's shape and color. Pay attention to any impressions you have as you attune with the image. Does it remind you of anything? What is the feeling that arises as you look at the flower? Write these things down.

Read about the patterns of imbalance and the harmonizing qualities for each card you pulled. Record any of the patterns of imbalance and harmonizing qualities with which you resonate.

Step 4: Use the Flower Essences

Use the corresponding flower essences. (See Chapter 9.) Keep the cards in a readily visible place while you are using them.

Step 5: Evaluation

Evaluate the effects of the flower essences when you have finished using them. (See Chapter 10.)

I have used your desert flower essences for the past eight years with important results. I thought I knew the essences really well, but now that I can see each flower I feel that a whole new understanding is happening.

~ A. B., California

I so much appreciate your flower cards. I have been using flower essences for a little over four years and I select them with a pendulum. Now, after I select a flower essence, I use the flower cards to see the actual flower. I feel much more connected to the flower itself and more connected to nature. The flower cards have taken me to another level of understanding the flower essences.

~ C. G., New York

Using Flower Cards in Groups

Using flower cards with two or more persons is fun and empowering. When using flower cards in a group setting, one person at a time selects the cards while the others provide support in consciousness by blessing the selector's process. There is an amazing grace in blessing others. It is a powerful thing to do with our personal will. You need not speak aloud. All you need do is think the highest thoughts for the person selecting the essences. You may want to think some of the following blessings to yourself:

- ❀ *May she/he find the deepest support possible for her/his intention.*

- ❀ *May he/she find the deepest peace and contentment.*

- ❀ *May this process bring him/her all that is most beneficial to his/her Highest good.*

Make up your own silent blessings while you support others in consciousness as they select the flower cards. It is a profound way to enhance the selector's intention.

When using flower cards in a group, you can use any of the above methods: the Attraction/Aversion Method; Flower Card Draw; the Flower Power Circle; Visual Attunement; or your own creative way.

I have been using desert flower essences off and on for about ten years. Even though I always have such good results with them, I tend not to take the time to select them for myself. I am rather a 'people person' and am more motivated when there are others involved.

After your workshop where you showed us how to use the flower cards, I went home and was inspired to initiate a monthly woman's circle. We get together on the first Sunday of each month and select flower essences together using the Flower Power Circle.

This process is so empowering, inspiring and supportive. We do follow-up in the beginning of the next meeting. And best of all, I now am using the flower essences in a more regular way, now that I have the group support. The whole group has asked me to write to you and extend our blessings for giving us this powerful gift.

~ W.K., Arizona

Using Kinesiology

Many folks rely on kinesiology, or muscle testing, to select flower essences. Muscle testing is the practice of using certain muscles of the body as an indicator for whether or not a substance is enhancing to your being.

Kinesiology is not one of the tools I use on a regular basis, but I have experienced it as an accurate method for selecting flower essences. Chiropractors and other alternative health care practitioners often use muscle testing. If you have had a practitioner ask you to hold out your arm as they pressed on it, you have probably experienced muscle testing.

There is a very simple way you can muscle test for flower essences without having another person to press your arm. It involves using the thumb and little finger of your left hand and the thumb and index finger of your right hand, if you are right handed. If you are left handed, you use the thumb and little finger of your right hand and the thumb and index finger of your left hand.

When you use kinesiology to select flower essences, strength indicates an essence that will strengthen you and weakness indicates something you don't need. The muscles of your fingers will remain strong or will weakly fall open when you test.

Following is a simple and well-known kinesiology method you can use yourself.

Finger Positions if You are Right Handed

Make a circle with the thumb and little finger of your left hand. Allow the tips of those two fingers to touch, completing an energy circuit. This is known as the circuit hand position (figure 4).

Extend your right index finger and thumb so they are parallel, and curl your other fingers under into your palm. We will call this the tester hand position (figure 5).

Insert the tester fingers into the circle on the circuit hand. Using the same amount of pressure to hold the fingers of the circuit together, press apart the tester fingers (figure 6). These hand positions might at first feel unusual or strange. Practice a little with holding your hands in these positions.

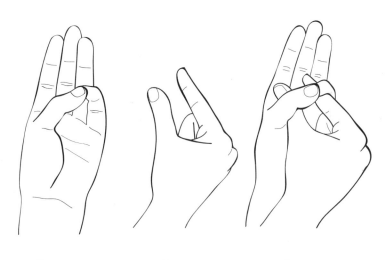

FIG. 4   FIG. 5   FIG. 6

Finger Positions if You are Left Handed

Extend your left index finger and thumb so they are parallel, and curl your other fingers under into your palm. This is called the tester hand position (figure 7).

Make a circle with the thumb and little finger of your right hand. Allow the tips of those two fingers to touch, completing an energy circuit. We will call this the circuit hand position (figure 8).

Insert the tester fingers into the circle on the circuit hand. Using the same amount of pressure to hold the fingers of the circuit together, press apart the tester fingers (figure 9). These hand positions might at first feel unusual or strange. Practice a little with holding your hands in these positions.

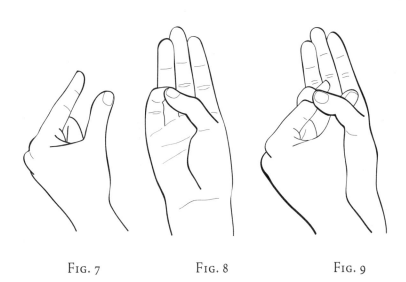

FIG. 7   FIG. 8   FIG. 9

Testing the Affirmative and Negative Response

Now, you can begin to use this method for testing. To make a test, ask yourself a question that has a very clear "yes" or "no" answer. You might ask yourself, "Is my name (whatever your name is)?" Insert the tester fingers into the circle on the circuit hand. Using the same amount of pressure to hold the fingers of the circuit together, press apart the tester fingers. The circuit hand position should remain strong. This is the affirmative response.

Test the negative response by asking a simple question that has a clearly negative answer. Insert the tester fingers into the circle on the circuit hand. Using the same amount of pressure to hold the fingers of the circuit together, press apart the tester fingers. The fingers should fall open weakly.

Like any new tool it takes practice to be comfortable with muscle testing. You mind will probably think it is strange, or weird, or might wonder if you are making either response happen. Three important things to remember are:

- ❀ You need to consciously apply the same amount of pressure on the circuit hand position as you do on the tester hand position.

- ❀ You need to consciously focus on what you are doing, and on the question or substance you are testing. Distractions may keep you from being accurate.

- ❀ Your hands will become tired at some point. If you get tired, you need to stop and rest your hands.

Selecting Flower Essences with Kinesiology

As with any other method for selecting flower essences, invoking your healing support team and defining your intention are essential if you want to be accurate in your testing. When you use these two steps before you use kinesiology, you will be able to accurately select the specific flower essences that match your intention. When the flower essence you are testing is in alignment with your intention, the circuit will remain strong.

Step 1: Intention

Invoke your healing support team. (See Chapter 6.)

Step 2: Invocation

Clarify your intention. (See Chapter 7.)

Step 3: Select the Flower Essences

When we use kinesiology to select flower essences it is helpful, but not essential, to have the essences in a kit box or some other container. If your flower essences are in a box or container, turn the bottles so that their labels are facing away from you and you cannot see the names of the essences. That way you will not be influenced by the names of the essences. If your flower essences are not in a box or container, arrange them randomly so that you cannot see the names.

If you have several boxes of flower essences, it is helpful to first test a box as a whole to determine whether there are any flower essences that correspond with your intention in that box. This process of elimination will save you time, and you will not have to muscle test each essence individually.

If you test strong for a box, and the box has two rows of flower essences, test to see if the essence or essences are in the top row, then the bottom row. Once you find the row, test each essence individually by asking if it is the first essence, the second essence, etc. The essences that test strong can be set aside as you continue.

Once you have tested all of the essences, write down the names of the ones you have selected. Then, engage your rational mind and study each essence to see if, and how, it applies to you. It is helpful to look up the harmonizing qualities and patterns of imbalance with which each essence works. Write down which patterns you recognize in yourself and which qualities you most want to enhance within yourself. Keep an open mind as you study the flower essence as there is usually a reason for the essence's appearance, even if you don't consciously understand it immediately. If you don't see the essence's relevancy, write this down as well.

Step 4: Use the Flower Essences

Use the flower essences. (See Chapter 9.)

Step 5: Evaluation

Always do a follow up session for yourself to evaluate the effects of using the essences. This will give you more confidence and will allow your mind to be engaged in the process. Evaluating the effects of using the flower essences is an important part of building confidence as you select flower essences intuitively. (See Chapter 10.)

If, after giving kinesiology a good try for a few weeks, you have a lot of difficulty or you just don't feel comfortable with this method, move on and try another of the selection methods in this book. Find the balance between learning a new tool and struggling with something that is not for you.

I use kinesiology to select flower essences. It is amazing to me how accurately the descriptions of the flower essences correspond. They are not the essences I would have picked using my mind, but they are always perfect for moving me along my inner journey.

~ A. R., Arizona

Using a Cross-reference

Another simple and easy method for selecting flower essences is using a cross-reference. A cross-reference, or repertory, is a list of harmonizing qualities or states of imbalance and the corresponding flower essences that work with those states. A cross-reference can be an important tool for selecting flower essences because it can quickly help you to find a flower essence to use.

For instance, if you find that you are often impatient and you want support, you can look up the word *impatience* in the cross-reference and find one or more flower essences that can help. Often you will find more than one flower essence because they will each address a different cause for the impatience, or different ways we have of expressing it. You then can read more about each of the flower essences and determine which one or ones best suit your particular impatience.

If you want to find the flower essences that will address the root of your issue, it is important to invoke your healing support team and define your intention before you use a cross-reference. This will enable you to be clear about what you want to change or work with.

When we use a cross–reference we usually look up a symptom, or the disharmony, with which we are uncomfortable. Often the symptom is a superficial manifestation of a deeper issue that we cannot see. By using the corresponding flower essence, we may find harmony with the symptom and also find that it uncovers something else. This process of "peeling the onion" is common in healing and evolving.

Another approach we might take when we use a cross-reference is to look up the quality that can harmonize the symptom or disharmony. Using the example of *impatience*, we might look up *patience* or *peace* instead and focus on the qualities that create harmony. When we define our intention, we will naturally identify the harmonizing qualities that we feel we need.

Whatever the approach you use, a cross-reference can be a valuable assist in selecting flower essences and learning more about the properties of each flower.

Step 1: Intention

Invoke your healing support team. (See Chapter 6.)

Step 2: Invocation

Define your intention. (See Chapter 7.)

Step 3: Select the Flower Essences

Select the flower essences using the cross-reference.

Step 4: Use the Flower Essences

Use the flower essences. (See Chapter 9.)

Step 5: Evaluation

Evaluate the effects when you are finished using them. (See Chapter 10.)

I have been using flower essences for about eight years. I have always used a cross-reference for selecting them. Before I learned about invocation and defining my intention, I would look up words that corresponded to the discomfort I was having and use the flower essences indicated. I had good success using the essences.

However, now that I define my intention and clarify the qualities I want to experience, the qualities are the words I seek in the cross-reference. I can say that my experience using the flower essences now is much more effective. I seem to move through my discomfort much quicker and I feel much more able to help myself. You have given me a tool for clarity. I am amazed at how this simple change in how I approach selecting the flower essences has provided me with a way to support myself in a meaningful way.

~ S. E., California

Chapter 9

———

STEP FOUR:
USING FLOWER ESSENCES

Earth laughs in flowers.
~ Ralph Waldo Emerson

THERE ARE SEVERAL WAYS in which to use flower essences once you have selected them. The most common way is to ingest them, a few drops, several times a day. A general guideline is to use them directly from the stock bottle, four drops in a small glass of water, once in the morning upon rising, and once in the evening before going to bed. You can also use them several other times throughout the day as you like.

Some folks like to skip the glass of water and take them directly into their mouth from the stock bottle. If you do this, you must be careful not to contaminate the glass dropper by touching it in your mouth.

There are also other ways that you can use flower essences. They are often effective when used topically. You can apply four drops to your palm and hold it over an area that you feel needs some support. One client who was recovering from sexual abuse mentioned that she was feeling an "energetic movement" in the area of her uterus. She had been releasing a lot of repressed anger and she sometimes felt as if her uterus was "vibrating" as a result. I suggested that she use the flower essences topically and "palm" her abdomen. After just two applications in this way the annoying feeling stopped and did not return.

Another client who has a degenerative disease of the central nervous system was scheduled to be traveling on airplanes for twenty-three days one particular month. She was concerned because her legs would twitch when she had to sit for long periods. She rubbed the flower essences we had selected into her legs during the long airplane journeys. She delightedly reported that her legs felt better than they had in three years, even with all the traveling. She also rubbed some of the flower essences over her liver area and reported that some congestion she had been feeling in one side of her body was much improved.

Flower essences can be sprayed into the air using four drops in a mister bottle filled with water. I worked with inmates in the state prison using this method for a period of one year with great results. I have worked with harmonizing the group dynamics in offices, homes, and other settings by using this application of flower essences. Misting flower essences in a room can change the energetic quality of the space. They can be used along with the principles of Feng Shui to enhance the qualities you want in a room.

How Long to Use a Flower Essence

I have experimented extensively with different approaches to using the flower essences. I often use a few drops of a flower essence just once to deal with an immediate need. Other times I find that I need to use the essence for a period of time.

I have found that there is a distinct cycle during which a flower essence, or a combination of essences, needs to be used to be fully effective. During this time we initially tend to use the flower essences more often and towards the end of the cycle less often.

To understand the cycle of using a flower essence, we can split it up into four parts.

The first part we can call "The Awakening". When we first begin to use a flower essence there is a growing of awareness of the situation, the issues, or the patterns of disharmony that we want to change. There is a hazy awareness, the promise of an insight not yet seen but on its way. In this part of the cycle, we usually have a natural urge to use the essence more often.

I tell my clients to use the flower essences as often as they want during the whole cycle. The majority of people report that they used them a lot at first, sometimes ten or more times each day during this first part of the cycle.

The second part of the cycle is when the awareness comes into focus or becomes clear. This second part I like to call "The Realization" or "Real-eyes-ation". Something about the issue is seen clearly for what it is.

The third part of the cycle is "Acceptance & Release". This is when we accept the issue, or pattern, and then release it. We can not resolve something until we fully embrace it. Once we accept the issue, we begin to experience harmonizing qualities that can help us let go of the mental or emotional charge that it has held.

The fourth part of the cycle is extremely important and is often undervalued because it is usually not as obvious as the earlier stages. The "Stabilization" stage is an integration, or fixation, of the qualities that the flower essence embodies. This is when the qualities are firmly established, and they then shine forth from us naturally.

Each person will have a specific cycle time that consists of these four stages. Each stage has its own length of time. Typically, we move faster through the first two stages, while the final two stages usually last longer in terms of chronological time. The graphic below shows a relative comparison of the approximate chronological time required for each stage.

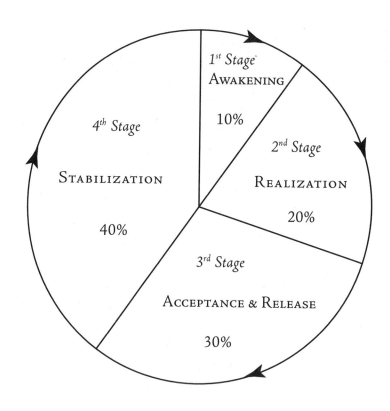

FIG. 10 – THE FOUR STAGES OF THE CYCLE

The importance of each stage is not in the length of chronological time that it takes to develop. Each stage is equally important. The fact that there is a difference in the length of time each stage requires is because they are psychological time, not chronological time.

Psychological time is related to the intensity of the remembrance. For example, if you are in an auto accident, the few seconds during the impact have a profound effect on what you remember. If you have to describe these few seconds, it will probably require more words and time than describing the following three hours. The impact of the experience psychologically has created a time warp: time has grown in relation to its psychological importance. There is a distortion of chronological time depending on the psychological impact the experience has had.

Many people remember the first and second stages of the cycle as more remarkable because the awakening and realization usually have a strong psychological impact. Insights can be instantaneous.

Both the "Acceptance & Release" and the "Stabilization" portions of the cycle usually take more time. We sometimes do not appreciate the time it takes to fully receive the changes and may even want to stop using the essence before this important part of the cycle is complete. We may think that we are complete with the essence because our awareness of the flower essence's action is not as dramatic, and we are tempted to move on before we are really finished. When we allow the proper amount of time for integration to take place, the changes facilitated by the flower essences will be stabilized.

In the beginning of the cycle, I encourage a client to use the essences as often as they want. Some clients use them seven or even as much as ten times a day at first. As the cycle progresses, people report that they take the essences less often and by the end of the cycle they find that they might be using them only once or twice a day. This is normal. As we use the flower essences and integration takes place, we become saturated with their qualities and we usually need to use them less often.

Each situation requiring the use of flower essences may have a different cycle time. We can say that a short cycle is less than one week, a medium cycle is one week to one month, and a long cycle time is more than one month. The majority of clients I see have a cycle time from two weeks to one month. Occasionally a short cycle time will be indicated, which usually prepares a client for a subsequent medium cycle.

There have been occasions when a client will need the same flower essence for a long period. In one particularly unusual situation, a client had the longest cycle time I ever saw. Marilyn, an extremely sensitive woman, recently came for a consultation after a period of seven years had passed since her last consultation. She told me that, odd as it may sound, she had been working with the combination of three flower essences we had selected during the consultation seven years previously. She, at last, felt ready for her next essences. She told me that she experienced many layers of changes activated by using the combination of flower essences. She was very conscious of the changes that happened, and she documented their effects carefully during the years. This was a very unusual situation. I more commonly find that long cycles last for one to three months.

How Do you Determine the Cycle Time?

There are several ways to determine how long to use the flower essences.

One way is through self-awareness. I like to encourage my clients to stay attuned to their inner process to see if they can recognize the cycle time as they use the essences. Many people can, especially after they have gone through a few cycles of using flower essences. It is an awareness that comes with experience.

As you use the flower essences, pay attention to what is happening. See if you can recognize the different stages as you use the essences. As you gain experience you will probably be able to recognize the cycle as it progresses, and you will soon be able to tell when it is finished.

When I work with my clients, I use a pendulum to find the cycle time. I suggest that they use the completion date as a guide, and I encourage them to develop the ability to sense when they are ready for the next set of flower essences by paying attention to their inner state. Most of my clients report that they easily learn to recognize their cycle time in this way.

The second way is to ascertain the cycle time using an intuitive method. You can use any of the methods discussed in Chapter 8: a pendulum, intuitive impression, or kinesiology.

Finding the Cycle Time Using a Pendulum

State your intention to find the most appropriate cycle time for the flower essences you just selected. The length of time to use the essences can vary from just one day to four or more weeks.

The easiest way to determine the cycle time using a pendulum is to use the Cycle Finder diagram included on page 118. Holding your pendulum in one hand, place one finger of your other hand in the box marked *1 - 7 Days* at the upper left side of the diagram. Check with your pendulum for an affirmative or negative response.

An affirmative response means that your cycle time is between one and seven days. Use your pendulum to check the circles to the right to ascertain the exact number of days.

A negative response indicates that you need to move on to check the *8 - 14 Days* box in the same way. Continue checking until you have found the appropriate time to use the flower essences.

If you test affirmative for the *More than 4 Weeks* box, it is recommended that you use the flower essences for four weeks and then test the cycle time again in the same way as above to see how much additional time is necessary.

Once you have found the cycle time, write it down.

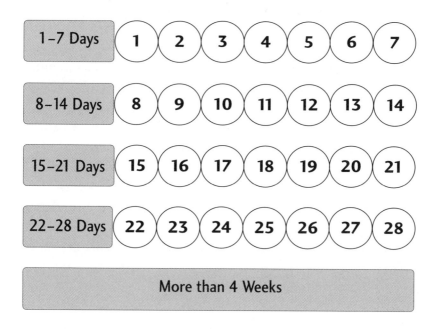

Fig. 11 – The Cycle Finder

Finding the Cycle Time Using Intuitive Impression

To select the length of time to use the essences with intuitive impression, hold your intention to find the most appropriate cycle time. Allow the number of days to intuitively appear within you and write it down.

Finding the Cycle Time Using Kinesiology

To select the length of time to use the essences with kinesiology, you can use the Cycle Finder diagram as a reference. Holding your intention to find the most appropriate length of time to use the essences, test if the cycle time is between one and seven days. If your response is affirmative, check each number between one and seven until you get an affirmative response. If the response is negative, test to see if the cycle time is between eight and fourteen days. Continue in this manner until you have found the exact number of days to use your flower essences.

If you test affirmative for more than four weeks, it is recommended that you use the flower essences for four weeks and then test the cycle time again in the same way as above to see how much additional time is necessary.

Once you have found the cycle time, write it down.

Using the "Default" Cycle Time

If you are not yet comfortable with an intuitive method for ascertaining the cycle time, use the essence(s) for a period of four weeks. This is a common length for a cycle.

You might ask, "What if I only needed them for three weeks and I used them for four?" You will do no harm by using the flower essences for a longer period than you need them because, if you no longer need the essences and you are still using them, nothing will happen.

You might also ask, "What if I need them for six weeks and I used them for only four?" In this case, if you use them for four weeks and then evaluate their effects, you might see that you have not yet resolved the goals that you set up when you defined your intention. At this point you might select flower essences again. If you still need to use one or more of the same flower essences longer, they will be indicated when you select your next set of essences.

Chapter 10

—

STEP FIVE:
EVALUATING THE EFFECTS

*Documenting and evaluating the flower essences' effects
deepens our understanding of ourselves.*

IF WE TAKE TIME TO EVALUATE the flower essences' effects, we may realize several important benefits. By taking the time to contemplate our experiences as we use the flower essences, we gain clarity about our inner life, our feelings, and our relationship with our Creator. Another benefit is that we often discover a new awareness of ourselves that becomes the foundation for selecting a subsequent set of flower essences.

Most people report that there were significant changes that happened after using the flower essences. Relationships became easier to deal with. Crisis situations were handled with greater peace. Many people report that a greater sense of their spirituality unfolded. Change was often met with greater ease. Some people found that their ability to recognize and let go of old attitudes and patterns was greatly enhanced. Emotional awareness and healing was heightened. These are just a few of the ways in which people notice the effects of the flower essences.

Sometimes when we use flower essences, the effects are quickly and dramatically obvious. At other times the changes they bring are subtle and not as easy to recognize. It is normal to have different experiences each time we use the flower essences. Don't worry if there are times when you can't see how the essences are working. It doesn't mean that you didn't do your part.

It takes careful contemplation to see how the essences have affected us. Sometimes it is necessary to have feedback from our friends and family members to help us see the changes that have taken place.

Many times a client will arrive for a follow-up session and say, "Well, I feel different, but I don't really see how the flower essences worked." When I refer to the notes I made when we selected the flower essences and remind my client of the issues that were a concern, she or he usually says, "Oh yes! That is no longer an issue. It just went away and I forgot about it!"

It is wise to systematically record our use of the flower essences so that we can have a reference from which to recognize their effects. In Chapter 5, I discussed the value of writing down certain key information before and after you select flower essences. Now, we will see how to use this information to evaluate how the flower essences have helped us.

Evaluating the Effects
During and After Using the Flower Essences

As you use the flower essences, write down any insights you have and any changes that you have experienced. You might jot down a few insights each day, or as often as you wish, while you are using the essences. When you have completed the cycle, it is a good idea to refer to the questions below and use them as a guide for evaluating the effects of the essences. If you did not see a change, write that down as well. Sometimes it takes the passage of time before we can recognize changes. Some changes are very subtle, and we recognize them only when someone mentions them to us or after we have completed another cycle of flower essences. It is helpful to write down the date when you record your insights.

Look at the comments you wrote after each flower essence at the time you selected them. Ask yourself questions based upon the comments about each essence that you wrote and the patterns of imbalance and the harmonizing qualities with which you identified. Be sure to record the date when you make follow up comments.

What are the things that we look for when we evaluate the effects of the flower essences? Following are a few questions that can help us evaluate the effect of using flower essences, whether for ourselves or for others:

1. How often did you use the flower essences?

2. What was your intention for using these particular flower essences? Were these goals met fully, partially, or not at all? If, for instance, one of the goals was to feel

peace, you might ask yourself if you are experiencing more peace in your life now.

3. Changing in consciousness often means a series of smaller changes in attitude that build upon each other. It is common for a flower essence cycle to resolve one or more layers necessary to achieve the ultimate goal. Can you tell if the flower essences resolved a part of the issue?

4. Did you experience a greater sense of self-acceptance? In what ways?

5. Can you or your friends notice any physiological changes in you, such as changes in your voice, posture, or your physical appearance?

6. Have there been changes in your body, such as a reduction of pain, soreness or stiffness?

7. Were there psychological or philosophical changes? Did you change your attitude about anything, either specifically or in a general sense? Did you make a change in the way you perceived yourself or the situation that provoked your use of flower essences?

8. Were there changes in any of your relationships or ways in which you related to others?

9. Did you experience lifestyle changes?

10. Were there any significant life events that happened during the cycle? What were they? Was your reaction to them different in any way?

11. Refer to the patterns of imbalance and harmonizing qualities that you recorded for each flower essence you selected. Did you notice anything in relation to these patterns or qualities?

12. Were there changes in yourself that are hard to define? Sometimes we can sense that something changed, but it takes the passage of more time before we can comprehend what it is and verbalize it.

13. Have the flower essences brought awareness of any new issues or further insights about existing issues?

14. After the name of each flower essence you used, list any patterns you became aware of and qualities that you feel have been enhanced.

It is helpful to contemplate the above questions and write down any insights you have. Don't worry if you are not clear about one or more of the questions. You might want to discuss your insights with your friend or support person to gain further clarity. Writing down your insights can create the foundation for the next cycle of flower essences. It will also help you gain confidence in your ability to select flower essences.

Flower essences work whether we consciously recognize their effects or not. Some folks may not want to take the time to document their process. This is fine and will not hinder the essences' effects. However, if we document and evaluate the flower essences' effects, it can deepen our understanding of ourselves, which is an important part of life.

Sample Documentation of a
Flower Essence Session

Date: *August 4, 2001*

1. What is going on that is provoking me to seek flower essence support at this time?

I realize that when I go out to lunch with my friends I tend to monopolize the conversation and talk about my problems. I am uncomfortable with this behavior but I don't know how to stop it. I feel nervous and I talk too much. On Tuesday, I had lunch with Angie. When I left, I realized that I had done it again; I talked the whole time and didn't really give her the space to talk about herself.

Also, I have what I call mini anxiety attacks, often in the evening when I return home. I think it is because I live alone and I feel like I might never have a mate.

2. What are the qualities that I think will help me with this issue?

- *Conscious of my needs and how to fulfill them*
- *Centered*
- *At ease*
- *Peace*
- *Self-acceptance*
- *Self-confidence*

3. Using the qualities I have selected, here are my goals with which I want flower essence help.

I ask for support in harmonizing the underlying cause of my incessant talking when I feel nervous.

I want to stop feeling so needy of attention from others as I feel centered in myself and self-accepting.

I want to feel comfortable when I am with others.
I want to feel self-confidence as I interact with others.

4. The Flower Essences Selected

I selected these flower essences, and I identified with the following patterns and qualities related to the essences.

INDICATED ESSENCES	PATTERNS OR QUALITIES & MY INSIGHTS
Milky Nipple Cactus	• needing constant attention from others
	• problems with the "mother connection"
	Wow, does this one describe me, with my continual problems in my relationship with my Mom, who wasn't there for me emotionally when I was a child and still isn't.
	• feeling as though you are dependent upon others
	I want to feel self-nurturing. I just don't know what I need and how to give it to myself.
Sow Thistle	• in social interactions with people this essence helps us deal appropriately with obnoxious behavior, whether it is our own or others'
	Yes! My own behavior feels obnoxious to me, and I am sure it is to others.
	• not giving others the space they need
	When I talk so much, it doesn't leave others any space to share.

5. The Cycle Time

Two weeks, until August 18, 2001

Sample Documentation of a Follow Up Evaluation

These comments were made after using the flower essences for fourteen days.

1. Date: *August 18, 2001*

2. How often did you use the flower essences?

At first I used them about six times a day. After about ten days, I used them about three times a day.

3. General insights after using the flower essences.

I felt myself become more grounded. I didn't realize how "out of my body" I had been until I had taken the flower essences for eight days. I realized that one way I deal with problems is to call my friends up and talk incessantly about how difficult these problems are. I hadn't realized how needy I am, and how I didn't seem to know what to do with this neediness. Milky Nipple Cactus seemed to help me with this.

I had a situation come up at work that required me to make a big decision. In the past I would have called up Sally or Joan and obsessed about it. But I didn't! I spent time on my own, being quiet and asking for the Universe to help me make this great decision. What a change! (Milky Nipple Cactus)

Amazingly, my Mom was easier for me to deal with these past two weeks. I saw that she treats me like a child, probably because I act like one. (Milky Nipple Cactus) I really want to work even deeper with this one. I feel like I am on my way, but I need further support with feeling like an adult when I am in my mother's presence. I think I'll use this as part of the focus for the next set of flower essences.

I still feel like I am dependent upon Joan, but it is easier for me to see that if I take a little time and ask for inner support, I can sometimes find what I need inside myself. (Milky Nipple Cactus) It doesn't work all the time, but at least seventy-five percent of the time I can now see that the answers are inside of me. I think I'll try a little experiment with myself and see if, when I feel that dependency feeling, I can just stop and ask myself what I need.

While using this essence, I became aware that I rarely take time to just sit by myself quietly. I always turn on the television when I am alone at home. In the car, I always have the radio to distract me. It felt nice to want to be quiet with myself. I am not sure which essence in particular helped me with this, but it feels great.

I could see that Sow Thistle helped me to be able to sit back and ask others how their day was, rather than needing to talk all the time about myself. I was able to consciously stop and think, "OK, now it is time to listen to Joan and how her day was and keep my mouth shut until she is done." I used to interject my own comments about myself whenever she would talk about something that happened to her, and I was much better about that.

Physically I felt much less nervous. I also stopped having my mini anxiety attacks I used to get, usually in the evenings when I return home. I feel a greater sense of calm, but I want to improve this even more.

These two essences helped me to see that I can help myself, but I feel I need further support in being able to recognize what my needs are. When I am in certain situations, I still feel that I am missing something. What support can I have that would help me to see my options in the moment? Also, now that I feel less nervous and a bit more calm around others, I see how much more I want to work with being even more confident in any kind of situation.

Here are the goals I had for these flower essences:

"Support in harmonizing the underlying cause of my incessant talking when I feel nervous."

This is much improved, but I want to deepen my ability to know what I need in the moment.

"I want to stop feeling so needy of attention from others as I feel centered in myself and self-accepting."

There has been a dramatic improvement here. I like being home alone, and I like being quiet and contemplating, rather than running about so much.

"I want to feel comfortable when I am with others."

I feel a great improvement with my close friends, but I want to feel more confidence with anyone.

"I want to feel self-confidence as I interact with others."

See above.

∞

Chapter 11

———

SELECTING FLOWER ESSENCES
FOR YOURSELF

The more we work with the flower essences,
the more we uncover our inner perfection.

LEARNING TO SELECT FLOWER essences for yourself can be a rewarding and self-empowering process. Sometimes it may be very easy, and at other times it may be challenging. Flower essences are safe to use. If you use a flower essence that you don't need, nothing will happen, so you can experiment with the flower essences with confidence.

One of the advantages when you select flower essences for yourself is that you don't need to wait for someone else to be available. You can be self-empowered.

Also, when you select flower essences yourself, you can learn to have a healthy detachment: you can experience your feelings and observe thoughts without "becoming" them. In this way you live in the world but are not of it.

131

A Few Challenges and Resolutions

There are several challenges we face when we select flower essences for ourselves. However, one of the beautiful things about selecting and using essences is that the process itself can overcome the challenges.

Perhaps the most important thing you need to have if you want to select flower essences for yourself is the willingness and the commitment to take responsibility for yourself and the situations in your life. You also need to have courage, determination, and some outside emotional support.

Following are a few challenges to selecting flower essences on your own and ways to resolve them:

❀ Self-confidence

❀ Remembering to ask for support

❀ Honesty with yourself

❀ Being too close to the issue to really see it

❀ Taking too much responsibility

❀ Reality check

Self-confidence

The process itself of selecting flower essences helps to build our self-trust and confidence. The more we work with the flower essences, the more we uncover our inner perfection and our self-esteem is strengthened. We do not need to have faith or believe in flower essences. We can see the results as we use them, if we take the time to look within ourselves. It is important to have a way to track our progress so we can clearly see what results we are having.

I like to use myself as a scientific laboratory. I experiment to see what effects I experience as I use the flower essences. I can see what the results are by writing down and then evaluating my experiences, and in this way I have the proving ground within myself. This attitude helped me uncover many delightful things about myself and gave me the opportunity to build my self-confidence.

Flower Essence Support

White Desert Primrose flower essence can help us have more confidence, especially when we feel self-doubt or confusion.

Remembering to Ask for Support

We need to remember to ask for support from the angelic realm, our healing guides and teachers. There is an endless amount of support available to us but it is not given unless we ask for it. By following the simple process in Chapter 6, you will automatically ask for support from the spiritual realm, and you will be guaranteed to receive it.

Another important kind of support is having a trustworthy friend, spouse, relative, or even a therapist to give emotional support. Having someone with whom you can talk is immensely important in the process of recognizing your inner state. It is important to ask for the support we need from other people.

You may find that you can confidently select flower essences for yourself until you come up against a particularly challenging situation in which you find it difficult to be objective about yourself. You may need to have the help of a professional practitioner or friend at this time, and then return to selecting the essences for yourself again at a later time.

Some people find it helpful initially to have several flower essence consultations with an experienced practitioner. This helps them recognize how the flower essences work and can help lay an excellent foundation for selecting flower essences for themselves.

Be willing to ask yourself what kind of support you need; then ask for it in the appropriate place.

Flower Essence Support

Giving & Receiving Support Formula™ is an excellent flower essence to use for helping us remember to ask for support.

Honesty with Yourself

The challenge of being honest with ourselves exists whether we select flower essences on our own or if we have the support of others. We have to be willing to go beyond denial and look with honesty at ourselves.

Sometimes it is difficult to stay with our process when we recognize things about ourselves that we do not like. It is helpful to remember that flower essences can help us accept ourselves, but be detached at the same time, as we move through the challenging situations. If you can view your process with a detached, but involved, attitude, it becomes interesting to see how everything will play out.

At any time you might ask yourself the following:

✽ Am I willing to confront myself?

✽ Am I being honest with myself about this situation?

✽ Am I committed to healing this issue?

✽ Am I ready to take responsibility for the situation?

✽ Am I being too hard on myself?

There is no right or wrong answer, just your own answer. No matter how you answer any of the above questions, you can congratulate yourself for having asked and answered them. You have given yourself the opportunity to be honest with yourself.

I remember at one time becoming aware that while I wanted to heal from a particularly painful experience, I wasn't yet ready to forgive one of the participants in the situation. I recognized my desire to forgive and also my unreadiness to do so. Just by being aware of this important aspect of the situation, and by accepting myself right where I was at that moment, I felt at peace with the situation, even though it was not yet complete. It took several years before I finally experienced the forgiveness that I had been hoping for. During this time, the unresolved situation did not have power over me, simply because I accepted myself.

Being honest with ourselves is not always difficult or painful. It takes practice. It also brings us face to face with the question of self-acceptance. If we experiment with being honest with ourselves and find that we are lacking in self-acceptance, we can select flower essences to deal with this immensely important aspect of our healing. You might set your intention to find the flower essences that will help you with self-acceptance, self-love, courage, and/or determination.

Flower Essence Support

Syrian Rue flower essence helps us to be honest with ourselves.

Too Close to See

One challenge when we select flower essences for ourselves is that we may be too close to a situation to see it objectively. When we talk with another person about it, we gain an outside perspective that can often give us insights into other ways of seeing, or framing, the situation.

When we use the five-step process and select flower essences with an intuitive method, this challenge can be overcome. If you select flower essences intuitively, you will be shown things about yourself that you may not have realized. When a particular flower essence is indicated, by reading its patterns of imbalance and harmonizing qualities, you might recognize and accept things about yourself of which you were previously unaware. We can sometimes accept certain things about ourselves when we are alone that we might not want to face if we are with another.

Flower Essence Support

Cane Cholla Cactus flower essence can help us if we are too close to our situation to be objective by helping us "leap" to a different perspective, seeing a situation with new eyes.

Taking Too Much Responsibility

When we work on our own, we sometimes become overly responsible for the situations and for our healing process. We may tend to take things too seriously or be too hard on ourselves. Sometimes we can even become "self-help addicts", constantly pushing ourselves in a way that is not harmonious. We need to inquire of ourselves whether we have an appropriate balance between taking responsibility for ourselves and being overly responsible.

We can sometimes recognize if we have become overly responsible if we find that there is a lack of joy in our lives. If we have difficulty laughing at our processes and ourselves, we are probably taking ourselves too seriously.

Fortunately the flower essences can help us with this. If you suspect that you have become too serious, you might check yourself by setting your intention to find what flower essences you might need to enhance self-love, joy, and play.

Flower Essence Support

The *Integrating Being & Doing Formula*™ flower essence composite formula is excellent for workaholics, even when it is self-help work that we are overdoing.

Reality Check

The people who use flower essences with themselves most successfully have an outer emotional support system that they use to gain a reality check. A trusted friend, relative, or professional can provide the support we need to recognize and process our reality.

When we spend a lot of time wrapped up in our inner world, we may lose touch with what is happening deeper within. Sometimes when we play over and over our thoughts and emotions, we cannot really see what is going on at a more profound level. We need a reality check, or a chance to talk things out. We might catch ourselves saying things that astound us. Often we find ourselves solving a problem by talking about it. All the rumination and contemplation is important, but the act of communicating makes movement: it can pull us beyond our thinking and reveal something deeper.

Sometimes when we recognize things inside that we think are ugly or unacceptable, we need to speak these things out loud to a person we trust. An unconditionally loving support person will give us the feedback that we are all right in spite of our perceived shortcomings. This is an important part of developing self-love.

Flower Essence Support

Mullein flower essence helps us if we wall ourselves off from others, helping us find support from sources that are truly supportive.

Chapter 12

———

FLOWER ESSENCE
SUPPORT CIRCLES

When we are truly compassionate,
we listen with our heart.

SELECTING FLOWER ESSENCES for yourself can be fun and empowering when you have the encouragement of one or more friends. It's amazing how powerfully we are supported when we allow ourselves to open up and share the intimate process of selecting flower essences with others whom we trust. Often, when we are in the midst of a healing process, it is difficult to know what we need, or even to know our inner reality. When we have a protected space in which we can talk freely, without judgement or censure, we find ourselves speaking truths about ourselves and clarifying what we feel and need.

Sometimes it can be helpful to hear an impartial view of our situation from another's perspective. A caring friend's viewpoint may lead us to a new awareness of a situation or process with which we are involved. We see that there are other ways to perceive a situation and this may inspire us to see ourselves differently. A caring friend may notice qualities that we have and are already using to cope with a difficult situation. Sometimes having someone notice our strengths shows us that we have what we need.

When we select flower essences with others, we can create a mutually supportive opportunity. Since each person has the chance to take turns being the listener and the one selecting flower essences, a sense of equality is created. A friend is not a therapist but a partner on the road to awareness.

You can create a flower essence support circle of two or more persons. There may be challenges, but there are also simple resolutions.

A Few Challenges and Resolutions

For some folks, interacting with others in a healthy way is natural. Others may experience one or more of the following challenges:

❀ Having good boundaries

❀ Giving support in consciousness rather than advice

❀ Maintaining a sense of balance

❀ Supportive feedback

❀ Honesty with yourself and others

Having Good Boundaries

Having good boundaries is a way of giving others the information they need to treat you with respect. The easiest way to create good boundaries when selecting flower essences with others is to discuss the purpose for selecting flower essences together. Why do you want to select flower essences with another? What kind of support would feel beneficial to you? What kind of interaction would you not want to have in this process? Contemplating and discussing these questions can help you create an intimate and supportive interaction.

Another thing to consider about boundaries is the place and time. To create a sacred circle with two or more persons, you need to select a time and place where you will not be interrupted by outside influences. Keep this time and place free from incoming telephone calls, others who need your attention, and any other distractions.

One key aspect of having healthy boundaries is to clearly understand compassion. Compassion is a deep feeling of sympathy for another who is experiencing an intense situation. Its opposite is indifference or mercilessness. A compassionate feeling is usually accompanied by a deep desire to alleviate another's suffering. This is natural, but we need to be clear about why we want to take away another's discomfort. Is it because we really want to help the other person, or is it because we feel uncomfortable with what we are witnessing? We must consider that change, transformation, and inner growth often come from uncomfortable situations and feelings. If we attempt to take away someone's discomfort, we might be depriving her or him of an important opportunity. If we have the ability to witness another's pain and suffering with sympathy, we can support inner growth and transformation.

When we are truly compassionate, we listen with our heart. By this I mean that, as we listen, we hear another's soul revealing the situations that provide the material of alchemy: the *stuff* of life whose resolution brings wisdom, understanding, and the grace of healing. Without these uncomfortable situations, we do not grow and transform. We need to respect another's discomfort so he or she can find awareness through resolving them. When we can view another's discomfort as if it is the grit in an oyster shell, we see that pearls of wisdom can result for our friends. In this way we let go of our need to take on, or change, another's pain or discomfort.

Flower Essence Support

Making & Honoring Boundaries Formula™ is the essence of choice for helping us with any kind of boundary issue.

Support in Consciousness

This is one of the most powerful ways in which we can support someone. Support in consciousness is simply supporting someone by listening and consciously acknowledging the support requested. What we focus on expands. When we provide support in consciousness, we focus on the qualities that someone wants to enhance in his life, and in this way we support him in manifesting those qualities.

Support in consciousness is not about judging or evaluating someone's situation. It is about seeing the highest possible blessing for a person, according to what that person wants. This is not a new concept or unusual practice. However, many of us forget the power that we have in blessing other people.

When we go to a wedding, we bless the union of two people who are marrying. When a baby is born, mother and father bless the baby, imagining a happy and healthy life for the child. When a friend is going through a rough time, we may envision her as supported by angels or as feeling safe and secure. Haven't you gone through a time that was difficult and felt like there was a supportive energy around you?

When we listen to a friend's process, we may have interpretations that are different from the one that she is making. It is important to detach from what we think about the situation. What we think about it is not really important. We may have a very clear insight about the situation that our friend is not yet ready to really hear. Or, we may have an insight that might apply if we were in the same situation but isn't applicable to our friend.

When we provide support in consciousness, we are not part of our friend's process except as a witness. We can anchor a peaceful and accepting state of being in which our friend can have her or his own experience. What we think about the other person's process is not important.

All we need to do is listen, to set aside any judgements we may have about our friend's process, and to support his or her intention. After all, no one knows what is best for your friends better than they do themselves. Your role is to honor them by consciously supporting their own desires. Your role is in providing an unconditionally loving space in which your friend can speak and hear her or his own inner wisdom.

How many times have you had the following happen? You see or sense something that seems obvious to you about a friend's process, and you tell her about it, perhaps even repeatedly. Then, a year later, she excitedly comes to you and tells you about a great revelation she had that is, in fact, the exact thing you told her about previously. We do not really hear something until we are ready. Even when we understand something intellectually, it might not sink into full awareness until the moment is really ripe. Only our soul knows when that time is at hand.

Each one of us has all the answers to our problems right within ourselves. No one else knows what is best for us. Even if you think that you see clearly what is needed for your friend, refrain from giving advice. When we give advice, it is based upon our perceptions and conclusions that result from our particular life experiences. It assumes that we know what is best for someone else. That is a great responsibility to assume. Even if it is common sense or intelligent advice, it might not be in alignment with what your friend needs to experience in relation to her issue. In this sense you can never know what is right for your friend, so it is much better to support her in finding the answer that feels right for her.

If your friend asks for advice, your best response is to ask her a question that will provoke contemplation. It is always appropriate to ask questions that might help her to ascertain the best answer from within herself.

If, for instance, your friend asks you, "What do you think I should do, go back to school or play it safe and keep my job?" You can ask questions like the following:

- If you go back to school, how will you feel?

- What are the advantages? The disadvantages?

- If you left your job, how would that feel?

- If you keep your job, will the comfort level it will provide be more important than the advantages of going back to school?

- If you go back to school, is it possible that something else can provide the feeling of safety that you need?

- What is motivating you to consider this opportunity at this time?

Questions such as these help your friend examine both sides of the issue and will eventually help her make her own decision.

Flower Essence Support

To help us give or receive support in consciousness, we can use *Unconditional Love & Support Formula*™.

A Sense of Balance – Giving & Receiving Support

In some friendships there can be a tendency for one of the friends to be the "needy" one and the other friend to play the role of caregiver. If this dynamic is present when you select flower essences, one of the two of you will ultimately not receive the highest support and the other will not have the opportunity to give. Giving and receiving are intertwined: one cannot exist without the other.

When you create a flower essence selection session, each person has the opportunity to play the role of the selector and the listener. To create equality, decide how long you want to spend together and divide the time equally between each person. Otherwise, you might find that you have spent all of the available time on one person and the other didn't get her chance. For instance, if you have two hours to spend and there are two of you, each person can have one hour for the selection process. If each person makes a commitment to honor the time element, everyone will feel secure in being able to have their needs met.

There is no right or wrong amount of time to spend in a flower essence selection session. You may spend one-and-a-half hours per person, or half-an-hour each. You can create the session as you wish.

Some things to consider about how much time you need:

1. How much time a person needs to reach clarity about what support they want form the flower essences. Sometimes it takes just a few minutes. At other times you may need half an hour just to process and clarify. In general, one hour should be abundant time for each person.

2. The method(s) you are using for selecting the essences and how comfortable each person is in using it. Each person can use their own method for selecting the flower essences. Some folks may need more or less time according to how proficient they are at using their favorite method.

3. Sometimes when a person is going through the steps of selecting the flower essences they may uncover a powerful insight or awareness of a deep healing process. There may be times when it is appropriate to allow some extra time for the process to unfold. It may be wise to factor in a little extra time for this possibility. Be aware if there is one person who always seems to need extra time. When we make a commitment to honoring the

---

Flower Essence Support

A great flower essence to enhance the flower essence circle experience is the *Giving & Receiving Support Formula*™.

Another flower essence that you might consider having all members of the circle use is called *Community Spirit Formula*™. This flower essence composite formula helps enhance the ability to sensitively and firmly express our personal needs in relation to the group and to contribute inspiration to the community.

group, as well as ourselves, we find that it is rare that extra time is needed.

4. When you meet for subsequent times, you will probably want to have some time for each person to follow up from the last session. Talking about the experiences we had after using the flower essences can help us to clarify how the essences worked.

Supportive Feedback

Feedback is a way of reflecting to another the perfection that already exists within her. It is not the opportunity you have been waiting for to correct another's perspective or try to change them. We reflect back to a person what we have heard them say.

It is always appropriate to give feedback based upon how you see your friend in the present moment. For instance, if you see your friend struggling with an issue, you might give the feedback that you see her courage in facing the issue. If you state your feedback in terms of the qualities you already see in her, it is a way of supporting and enhancing those qualities. It is empowering for the person to know that her qualities are apparent. Often, she herself doesn't notice them, so it is an opportunity for you to acknowledge her strengths. It is not helpful to make things up and say pretty words that have no real meaning. Rather, look at your friend with the intention of seeing the qualities she is already exhibiting. They are always there, and they are always important to notice.

Be conscious of the time when you are giving feedback. It is easy to get carried away and take up more time than might be necessary. Be aware that you are participating in the time allotted to your friend. Don't attempt to process your own issues while giving feedback to another. If you keep it concise and based on the qualities you see in your friend, your feedback will probably be supportive.

When giving feedback it can also be supportive to ask contemplative questions of your friend. They are not questions that require an answer in the moment, but rather questions that, if your friend chooses to contemplate, might help her find the answers she is seeking inside herself.

Flower Essence Support

The *Unconditional Love & Support Formula*™ can be used to enhance our ability to give supportive feedback.

Honesty with Yourself and Your Friends

There may be certain issues that you will not be able to remain impartial about with a friend. If this is the case with a particular issue your friend is dealing with, you might have to excuse yourself from offering any feedback about that issue. It requires a lot of honesty with yourself to recognize when you are "hooked" by something your friend is speaking about. How do you know if you are hooked?

1. You are unable to remain impartial about a certain subject or situation.

2. Feelings arise that keep you from being able to focus your attention on the other person. These feelings may be strong or insistent, indicating that you have unresolved issues.

3. You feel certain that you have the right answer to your friend's situation.

If you recognize that you are hooked by something, it is appropriate to refrain from offering feedback. When your turn comes to select the flower essences, you may wish to use this as a focal point for your own flower essences, or you might want to wait a while and process on your own until you want support with it.

Flower Essence Support

When we have difficulty being honest with our friends or ourselves, we can use *Syrian Rue* flower essence.

How to Create a Flower Essence Support Circle

Two or more people can create a sacred healing circle in which each person can clarify his or her needs and select the most beneficial flower essences. The participants can be pure mirrors for each other's true nature and reflect back to each other the qualities they see.

The Participants

When creating a flower essence support circle, look for one or more persons who:

❀ Engender trust.

❀ Listen when you speak.

❀ Do not give advice, but who ask contemplative questions of you.

❀ Commit to confidentiality.

❀ Are punctual and dependable.

❀ Notice the changes you have attained and applaud your successes.

❀ Honor you, and your process, just as you are.

The Roles

Each session is a sacred healing circle in which the person selecting flower essences has the opportunity to ask for support and the listener(s) can offer support in consciousness. Following are the guidelines for the two roles everyone gets to play in the circle: the selector and the support person. A dynamic support opportunity can be created for everyone when all participants understand and commit to these roles.

The Selector's Role

❀ To contemplate and ascertain what support you would like to receive from the flower essences you are about to choose.

❀ To honor the established time frame.

❀ To receive support in consciousness from the support circle.

❀ To honor the confidentiality of the session.

The Support Person's Role

❀ To hold the sacred energy of the healing circle.

❀ To listen with an open heart.

❀ To abstain from giving advice or trying to fix the selector.

❀ To provide support in consciousness by focusing 100% attention on the selector.

❀ To honor the established time frame.

❀ To honor the confidentiality of the session.

When to Meet

Some groups like to meet more often than others. Very often a group will choose to meet once a month. This makes it easy for participants to find the time, and once a month is easier for many people to manage.

Meeting once a week, or once every two weeks, can provide an opportunity for the participants to "check in" emotionally. Even if a participant's flower essence cycle is not complete, and she is not ready to select new flower essences, it gives a chance to verbalize what has been happening and have a reality check. It can also be an opportunity to simply support others in consciousness and experience the joy of heart-centered connection with others.

How often you meet is up to you as a group. Your commitment to the meeting time is important and will create a stable foundation for the circle.

A Flower Essence Support Circle Format

Following is a format for setting up the circle. You can use it as it is, or adapt it to fit your own group.

1. Set up a time and place where you will be able to have a flower essence session together without being disturbed or interrupted.

2. Decide how long you want to spend and divide the time equally between the number of participants in the circle. It is helpful to have a clock easily visible. You might select a person to keep track of time and remind others if they need it. Then decide who will be the first to select the flower essences.

3. The person whose turn it is to select essences can invoke her healing team. (See Chapter 6.) This can be silent or aloud, however she is comfortable.

4. The selector spends some time talking about what is happening that is creating the desire to have support from the flower essences. She can be as specific or as broad as she wants. There is no right or wrong way, just each person's own way to create clarity. If this is a follow up session, she might summarize her experiences from using her last set of flower essences. She might explore any new awareness that they brought her, as well as clarify what she wants the new flower essences to address. The selector might ask herself questions such as:

❧ What is happening in my life?

❧ What sort of discomfort or challenging situation am I facing in my life?

❧ In what way do I want to be different?

❀ How do I want to feel, compared to how I am feeling?

❀ What qualities do I want to enhance in myself?

5. The selector writes down her intention for the essences she wants to select. (See Chapter 7.) She can do this before the circle meets or at this time, whichever is more comfortable and convenient.

6. The selector then selects the flower essences using her favorite method: flower cards; a pendulum; kinesiology; a cross-reference; or any other method. She might also read about each essence she selected and, in a few words, discuss how it might apply for her.

7. If she wants, she can ask for supportive feedback from the listener(s). This is optional and completely up to the selector.

8. The next person takes her turn.

9. When all the persons have completed their turns, decide when and where to meet again.

10. Close the circle by closing your eyes and allowing yourselves to feel gratitude for the support you have received from nature and your friends.

Chapter 13

——

Selecting Flower Essences
for Others

*There are times when we can be
of genuine help to others...*

ALL FAMILY MEMBERS, young and old, and even pets and animals, can safely use flower essences. There are situations when someone may want to use flower essences but is not able to select them. A few examples are: children; those who do not have confidence to select flower essences for themselves and are not yet ready or willing to learn; those who are incapacitated; in emergency situations; and pets and animals. Many people who want to try flower essences for the first time often prefer that someone else select the essences for them.

When we select flower essences for others, we act as a support person. No one knows what is best for someone else. Even a mother with a newborn intuitively attunes with the baby to ascertain his or her needs; the information comes from the baby. The art of selecting flower essences for others lies in our commitment to being a support person for another and continually searching for ways in which we can draw out another's own innate healing wisdom.

In almost every flower essence seminar I have given, questions arise such as the following: "My husband is so judgmental, what flower essence can I give him?" "My mother is so invasive in my affairs all the time. What flower essence can I give her to make her stop?" "What flower essence can I give my son, who is unmotivated?"

When we have a problem with another's behavior, it is just that: *our* problem. When we focus on what flower essences *we* need in that situation, most often the other person will change, your behavior will change, or their behavior will no longer bother you. If we want to select flower essences for someone else because we want to change him or her, we would better serve that person by focusing on ourselves, and select the flower essences to help ourselves.

Another common comment goes something like this: "And by the way, he doesn't want to take flower essences so I sneak them into his orange juice in the morning." From my perspective, it is not supportive to sneak flower essences. If others do not want to use them, you might consider this as the wisdom of their soul speaking to you. They really do know better than you do about what is best for them. Flower essences may not be right for everyone, or might not be right at this time. It is important that when we select flower essences for others it is with their permission.

The best way to show others how helpful the flower essences are is to use the essences yourself, and just let others notice the improvements.

I remember one woman who wanted her husband to use flower essences. She told him about them but he was not interested. She wanted me to show her how to make him use them. I suggested that she just let go of her desire to have him use the essences and focus on herself. She began to have flower essence consultations once a month, and also selected some flower essences herself as she felt she needed them.

Seven months later I had a phone call from her husband requesting a flower essence consultation for himself. He said, "I am so impressed with the changes in my wife that I want to see if the flower essences can help me with a situation that I am dealing with at work. I never thought flower essences could help make the deep changes that I see in my wife."

Every relationship is a mirror of our own selves. What we see in others reflects the relationship we have within ourselves. If we see something in someone that we don't like, we can use flower essences to help us change ourselves. This is one way in which we can empower ourselves. If you are not sure if this really works, don't just take my word for it. Try it sometime. Use yourself as an experiment.

There are times when we can be of genuine help to others by selecting flower essences for them. Perhaps you can tell when a friend genuinely wants to deal with the underlying cause of a situation. You may feel inspired to mention the flower essences and how they helped you. It is important to listen to their response. If they are really interested, they will say so.

Sometimes flower essences are an important modality for someone, but you are not the most appropriate person to help them. Selecting flower essences for family members or friends can sometimes be challenging. It is important to check with yourself first to see if you are comfortable in this role. Here are a few things you can contemplate to determine if you want to support others in this way.

What is Motivating You?

How do you tell if you can be a support to others with the flower essences? Perhaps the first question to ask yourself is whether the other person really wants to use the flower essences, or whether you are projecting your own discomfort onto him.

Other questions you might ask yourself are:

❀ Why do you want another person to use flower essences? Is it because you want to change him? Or do you feel a sense of compassionate detachment from his situation?

❀ Do you feel that you are the only one who can help him? Or do you want to help him to help himself?

❀ Is the issue with which the other person is working one that is *loaded* for you? By this I mean, is the issue something that provokes strong feelings within you that keeps you from being able to be one hundred percent present as an observer? As this person speaks, do strong feelings arise that you need to process yourself?

❀ Do you think that you already know what the other person needs? ("Oh, if she would just *leave* that guy, her troubles would be over!")

❀ Do you feel that you *have* to do it? Is it an obligation?

❀ Do you feel too involved in the other's life in a way that keeps you from being detached?

The answers to these questions can reveal your motivation behind your desire to help another. If you always keep the attitude that you are supporting others and that you are not an authority on what is best for them, you will probably be able to help others with flower essences.

Following are a few important and desirable qualities to have in order to support others:

- ❀ Clarity about your motive and intention for helping others with flower essences.

- ❀ Consciousness of appropriate boundaries.

- ❀ Honoring confidentiality.

- ❀ Being a peaceful listener and observer and offering support in consciousness.

- ❀ Compassionately honoring the other's perspective and state of being.

Flower Essence Support

Red Root flower essence helps us to be conscious of our motives, bringing us perception that escapes cultural conditioning and prejudice.

Making & Honoring Boundaries Formula™ is excellent for helping us with all issues of boundary making.

Unconditional Love & Support Formula™ is excellent for enhancing true compassion and acceptance of others, helping us to honor others.

Children

Children respond very quickly and well to flower essences. I have seen amazing changes in their behavior and emotional responses. Most children seem to have a natural affinity with flower essences. We have a responsibility as parents to provide the best support possible for our children. Flower essences can provide the harmonizing grace that can change the root of behavior or thoughts that hamper a child.

I remember a two-and-a-half year old who had tremendous temper tantrums. After she used flower essences for three days, they completely stopped. Her mother told me that her daughter called the flower essences her "happy drops" and would remind her mother to give them to her throughout the day. About eight months later her mother went through a divorce. Her daughter told her that she needed some more "happy drops" because she was starting to feel "fuzzy."

Another child, who had been using flower essences from time to time since she was eighteen months old, told her mother, "I need to go and see Cynthia for flower essences because I am beginning a new school year. There will be new children and I want to feel good about making new friends." She was seven years old at the time, and already she knew that the flower essences provided her an emotional support that she wanted.

One woman who is a counselor and flower essence practitioner reported the following: "A few months before my daughter was to turn three years old, she started having emotional fits of frustration with herself: throwing herself on the floor, crying, and saying, 'I can't do it. I stupid.' These fits occurred every time she was unable to manipulate an object, draw something, explain something to someone, or perform some physical act. It was as if she could not meet up to her own high expectations of herself, as if she felt trapped in a two-year-old body with its limitations.

"I did a flower essence attunement with her and she attuned strongly to Teddy Bear Cholla Cactus and Candy Barrel Cactus. I find humor in how fitting these names are for a small child.

"I witnessed an immediate change in her on the first day. Her reactions to previously frustrating situations were now calm and reasonable. She would ask for help instead of crying and saying negative statements about herself. She showed more patience with her clumsy little body and her limited vocabulary.

"After a few days, when I had forgotten to administer the essences regularly, she came to me in tears asking for 'the drops' and saying she was 'getting too upset with myself.'

"She continued to ask for the drops on occasions over the next few months. She began to verbalize more positive self-statements such as, 'I'm just learning.' and 'When I'm bigger I can do it.' Her new found patience allowed her to do more problem solving, so she actually could achieve more."

Another woman sent me the following story: "One woman I know has a grandchild named Jessica who has a tendency toward an attention disorder. This introverted child never spoke to people in the neighborhood. Her grandmother gave her Fairy Duster flower essence, several times a day.

"Three days later, the child noticed a neighbor and asked, 'Who are you?' Within five days the child was interacting with the neighbors, which was a remarkable change."

I have seen great changes in behavior with children of all ages, including teenagers. By the time kids are teenagers they can often select the essences for themselves or with friends.

When we select flower essences for children, we define the intention for the essences ourselves, because children are not usually able to verbalize their inner state. Some children love doing the selecting themselves by using flower cards, with the flower power circle method or the attraction/aversion method. Alternatively you can use any of the methods in this book to select the essences for them.

To give the flower essences to a child, you can simply add four drops of each essence to a little bit of water and have the child drink it. You can also use four drops of each essence on your hands and then gently stroke the child. This is a great way to use flower essences with infants.

Pets & Animals

I have received feedback from folks who use flower essences with horses, dogs, cats, guinea pigs, birds, and pigs. Animals respond very quickly to flower essences, and it is comforting to know that we can support them in such an easy way.

An easy remedy for an animal in many cases is the *Crisis – Desert Emergency Formula*™. This flower essence has been shown to have a very calming effect for animals and birds and often is the only essence needed. However, there are challenging situations that call for selecting other flower essences.

There are animal sanctuaries that have reported that they use the *Crisis – Desert Emergency Formula*™ when the animals are first brought to them. It helps them adapt more quickly. Also, *Milky Nipple Cactus*, a flower essence that works especially well for abandoned animals or persons, is often used.

One woman asked me to select flower essences for two of her cats. Toby had been abandoned, and was now a street cat. My client used to put food out for him, to which she added flower essences to help build trust. After a short time she brought him home.

Things went along well with his adjustment to a domestic life, and my client was impressed with how much the flower essences helped. Then, when she brought home another stray, a war broke out. She had to keep the two cats in separate rooms because the new cat, Tiger, who was of a very jealous nature, would fight with Toby. She gave Milky Nipple Cactus to Tiger and it calmed him down immediately.

However, Toby was now hiding out all the time, and the situation was worsening. Three flower essences were indicated for Toby: Desert Holly, Cane Cholla Cactus and Morning Glory Tree. Desert Holly is used for those who run away from love, either out of a fear of being smothered or a fear of being unloving. We use Cane Cholla Cactus for overly defensive behavior and for helping us have a new perspective of a situation. Morning Glory Tree is an essence that helps us when our behavior is ancestral and addictive in nature. My client told me that she had seen Toby's mother and that she knew the mother abandons her babies.

After two weeks, both of the cats tolerated each other. Toby stopped hiding, and Tiger stopped attacking. After two months had passed they would sometimes curl up and sleep together.

Working with pets and animals is very much like working with children. Invoke your healing support team and define your intention based upon what support you think the animal needs. Then select the flower essences using your favorite method.

One way to administer flower essences to animals is to add drops of each essence to the animal's drinking water. Or, you can put four drops of each flower essence on your hand and gently pet the animal, especially down its spine, if possible.

Working with Plants

I have used flower essences with plants with some good results. A friend of mine had several plants that were obviously not happy. They were drooping and looked as if they lacked vitality. She tried watering them more, watering them less, repositioning them to receive more light and then less light. She tried different kinds of plant food and repotted them, but nothing made any difference.

Before she threw them away, I suggested that we try watering them with *Crisis – Desert Emergency Formula*™, a composite of essences that has been shown to be very effective in many different situations. After one week the plants had a slight improvement. After the second week they looked noticeably more vibrant. At the end of the third week there was new growth beginning. Fifteen years later they are still thriving.

I don't understand how or why these plants responded to the Crisis Formula, but the effects were remarkable.

Chapter 14

—

Working with a
Flower Essence Practitioner

It's a blessing to allow yourself to receive support.

THERAPISTS OF MANY TYPES are now incorporating flower essences into their work. Many psychologists, spiritual counselors, psychiatrists, social workers, dentists, doctors, chiropractors, massage therapists, and others are now using flower essences in their practices. Others are encouraging their clients to use them on their own or with the help of a flower essence practitioner. These are practitioners whose main focus is on helping you to achieve clarity about what support you want to have and then selecting the flower essences to enhance your intention.

It can be important to have professional support for selecting flower essences. When you are in the midst of a great transformation, if you are involved in a healing process that is very intense and you are not clear or sure of how to support yourself, you may want to work with a professional. Some of us have healing projects that we have been working with for a long time and have become "stuck" in our perception of the process. To help us reach a new perspective on our process, we might consider the help of a flower essence practitioner.

A professional can have a more impartial view of you than a friend or relative. A good practitioner can help create a safe and supportive space in which you can process. This sacred space can give you permission to step outside of how you normally view yourself and give you an opportunity to view yourself from a new perspective.

You might be willing to share more intimate things with a professional practitioner than you would with a friend or relative. Also, an experienced practitioner may have personal and professional experience in resolving the same, or similar, issues that you are attempting to harmonize. There is an important power in knowing that someone else has been successful in dealing with the same issues with which you struggle.

When we work with a professional, we are often more serious about our commitment to resolving our problems and finding healing harmony. For some people, the formal setting and time commitment help them place a higher value on the support.

When you use flower essences, the harmonizing and subtle effects often solve the problems without your noticing. It is common that folks say, "Yes, I took the essences, I feel better, but I don't know if they really worked." A good practitioner will be able to ask you questions that can help you evaluate the process of using the essences. He or she can also be a cheerleader, supporting you in your inner efforts and helping you to help yourself.

If you decide to work with a flower essence practitioner, or any type of professional who uses flower essences, the most important thing is to find someone with whom you feel good. The trust that evolves between you and your practitioner is very important to your healing process. A session with a flower essence practitioner is usually an intimate opportunity to help you see what is happening within yourself and become clear about what it is you want to change or harmonize. Trust develops over time, but your initial feeling about a practitioner is important.

It is good to question a professional about any concerns you have. A practitioner with integrity will honor confidentiality, appointments, and conduct the session in a way that honors you. Good practitioners will know their limits and refer you to someone else if they do not feel that they can help you, or if they recognize that someone else could support you better.

It is important to follow the initial two steps we have discussed in the previous chapters when you work with a practitioner of any sort. The initial steps are just as important when you have a professional consultation as when you select the flower essences alone. It is best to take time before a session to invoke your healing support team and write down whatever you can to clarify your intention. When you speak with your practitioner, you will probably find that you will go even deeper and have more clarity about the situation. When you prepare for a session by doing these two steps, you will help create a powerful healing circle, and you will empower yourself as an active participant in your healing process.

If you didn't manage to do the initial two steps before your session, do them in the session itself. If you are not comfortable invoking your healing team aloud, do it silently in the waiting room, or ask your therapist for a moment of silence while you invoke support. Defining your intention can be done together with your practitioner.

On the next page are some items to consider when you prepare for a follow-up session with a flower essence practitioner.

Feedback to Give Your
Flower Essence Practitioner

1. The experiences you had while using the flower essences.

2. What other therapies or healing modalities you used during the cycle time.

3. Any significant life events that happened during that time, even if they seem unrelated to using the flower essences.

4. Any insights you had, whether they seem related to the flower essences or not.

5. Any awareness of new issues that have surfaced.

6. Any specific insights you had about a particular flower essence you used.

See Chapter 10 for more information and support.

Common Questions asked of
Flower Essence Practitioners

Will flower essences interfere with other healing modalities?

It has been our experience that flower essences are safe to use with other healing modalities. They seem to enhance other therapies, bringing us an added support on the emotional and spiritual levels that may be missing in other therapeutic approaches.

Over the past eighteen years, a number of psychiatrists, psychologists, medical doctors, and alternative therapists of many types have referred their patients to me for flower essence support. Many of these professionals have remarked that the patients who use flower essences in addition to their other therapy heal much faster than those who do not use flower essences.

One psychologist who specialized in recovery from drug and alcohol addiction told me that the patients that she sent to me, and who consistently used flower essences, processed and healed at a much faster rate then those who didn't. She told me that every one of her patients who used the flower essences resolved issues and moved on with their lives in a self-empowered way.

I view flower essences as a complementary therapy that can be safely added to other healing modalities.

Can I use any other essences during the time I am using the selected essences?

Each practitioner may feel differently about this, so it is good to ask your practitioner this question if you feel a need to use another flower essence during the cycle time. I personally feel that it is all right to use another essence in addition to essences recommended, if you feel you really need it. However, it is very important to tell your practitioner what essence you used and how often you used it, and any effects you noticed from its use, so that she or he can document and use it as part of the evaluation process. I find that during particularly intense healing opportunities my clients sometimes need the *Crisis – Desert Emergency Formula*™ in addition to the indicated essences. This flower essence helps them stay "in the moment" and present with their healing process. The essence can be used as often as you want.

How can I enhance my understanding of the flower essences I am using?

Three great tools to enhance your experience with the flower essences are: a good book describing the flower essences you are using; flower cards or photographs of the flowers themselves; and a pen and notebook or journal. See *Appendix A: The Flower Essence Journal.*

It can be immensely helpful to read about the flower essence as you are using it. Read about the flower essence several times during your cycle of use. Formulate questions about the harmonizing qualities and the patterns of disharmony. Ask yourself, "Am I experiencing this pattern or quality?" If you can spend just fifteen minutes a day, perhaps in the evening or whenever you have quiet time, contemplating and writing down your insights, you will enhance your experience of using the flower essences.

When life events happen, contemplate the flower essences you are using. Do you recognize any of the patterns of imbalance or the harmonizing qualities in how you are reacting to the situation?

See if the flowers have something to show you. When you look, the secrets of nature are openly revealed. If you have a deck of flower cards or a picture of the flower, place it where you can see it from time to time throughout the day, or during your quiet time. You can dialog with the flower, asking to be shown how its qualities can be, or are being, integrated within you. When you ask, you always receive. Don't forget to listen once you ask!

Writing down insights or how you are feeling as you take the flower essences can reveal surprising things to you. Even if it is just a few minutes each day, or ten minutes once a week, contemplating and writing can open you to your inner world.

The Flower Essence Journal in Appendix A can guide you through questions that will help provoke you to understand your inner process.

Appendix A.

———

THE FLOWER ESSENCE JOURNAL

This journal lays out five steps for selecting and using flower essences. For further information about each step, please refer to the corresponding chapters. For in-depth information on the patterns and qualities of each desert flower essence, you can refer to *The Alchemy of the Desert*, by the same author.

This journal can be used to select flower essences for yourself. If you are selecting flower essences for others, it is recommended that each person have his or her own journal. The journal can help folks clarify their issues before a consultation and support their ability to recognize the flower essences' effects for a follow-up consultation session. These journal pages can also be downloaded from the web site at: www.desert-alchemy.com.

Following are a few qualities to which that you might want to refer when you define your goals and intention. You can add other qualities to this list as you are inspired.

❀ clarity   ❀ abundance
❀ focus   ❀ gentleness
❀ love   ❀ selflessness
❀ healing   ❀ harmlessness
❀ wisdom   ❀ calmness
❀ deliverance   ❀ centeredness
❀ joy   ❀ groundedness
❀ playfulness   ❀ unity with God or the Creator
❀ humility   ❀ bliss
❀ compassion   ❀ gratitude
❀ understanding   ❀ enthusiasm
❀ integrity   ❀ patience
❀ tenderness   ❀ humor
❀ creativity   ❀ delight
❀ mercy   ❀ _____
❀ kindness   ❀ _____
❀ goodness   ❀ _____
❀ benevolence   ❀ _____
❀ holiness   ❀ _____
❀ full self-expression   ❀ _____
❀ purity   ❀ _____
❀ warmth   ❀ _____
❀ balance   ❀ _____
❀ sacredness   ❀ _____
❀ blessedness   ❀ _____
❀ peace   ❀ _____
❀ harmony   ❀ _____
❀ generosity   ❀ _____

Name: _____

Date: _____

Step 1. Invocation

(See Chapter 6)

Invoke your healing team.

_____
_____
_____
_____
_____
_____
_____
_____
_____
_____
_____
_____
_____
_____
_____
_____
_____
_____
_____
_____

Step 2. Defining Your Intention

(See Chapter 7)

A. What is provoking you to want flower essence support at this time? Write about what is creating discomfort for you right now.

_____

_____

_____

_____

_____

_____

_____

_____

_____

B. What are the qualities that you want to enhance that will help you with this issue? See list on first page.

_____

_____

_____

_____

_____

_____

_____

_____

C. Using the qualities you selected above, write down one or more phrases that indicate the goals with which you want flower essence support.

_____

_____

_____

_____

_____

_____

_____

_____

_____

_____

_____

_____

_____

_____

_____

_____

_____

_____

_____

_____

_____

_____

_____

_____

_____

_____

_____

_____

_____

Step 3. Selecting Flower Essences

(See Chapter 8)

Select the flower essences using your favorite method. Write down the essences you have selected. Refer to *The Alchemy of the Desert* and read about each essence selected. Next to each essence write down one or more of the patterns of disharmony that seem true for you. You can also record any harmonizing qualities that you feel would help you. Also, record any of your own insights about how you think this essence might help you.

essences selected	patterns of imbalance & harmonizing qualities
_____	_____
_____	_____
_____	_____
_____	_____
_____	_____
_____	_____
_____	_____
_____	_____
_____	_____
_____	_____
_____	_____
_____	_____
_____	_____
_____	_____

essences selected

patterns of imbalance & harmonizing qualities

Step 4. Using the Flower Essences

(See Chapter 9)

Cycle Time (length of time to use the essences): _____

Insights about yourself and your inner and outer processes as you use the flower essences:

date	insights
_____	_____
_____	_____
_____	_____
_____	_____
_____	_____
_____	_____
_____	_____
_____	_____
_____	_____
_____	_____
_____	_____
_____	_____
_____	_____
_____	_____
_____	_____
_____	_____
_____	_____

date   insights

Step 5. Evaluating the Effects

(See Chapter 10)

Date: _____

How often I used the flower essences: _____

_____

_____

_____

_____

Essences used: _____

_____

_____

_____

_____

_____

_____

_____

_____

_____

_____

_____

_____

_____

_____

_____

General observations about myself since using these flower essences:

_____

_____

_____

_____

_____

_____

_____

_____

_____

_____

_____

_____

_____

_____

_____

_____

_____

_____

_____

_____

_____

_____

_____

_____

_____

_____

_____

Significant events that happened during this time:

_____

_____

_____

_____

_____

_____

_____

_____

_____

_____

_____

_____

_____

_____

_____

_____

_____

_____

_____

_____

_____

_____

_____

_____

_____

List each essence and discuss whether you noticed any of the patterns of imbalance, the harmonizing qualities, or other insights about that particular essence.

essence used   insights, patterns, and qualities I noticed

—

Flower Essences
Mentioned in this Book

Flower Essence Composite Formulas

A Way to the GodSelf Formula 54

Community Spirit Formula 146

Crisis – Desert Emergency Formula 26, 162, 164, 169

Deepening Inner Union Formula 57

Emotional Awareness Formula 34, 37, 66, 70

Giving & Receiving Support Formula 56, 134, 146

Integrating Being & Doing Formula 137

Making & Honoring Boundaries Formula 86, 142, 159

Saguaro-Queen Formula 35, 37

Unconditional Love & Support Formula 145, 148, 159

Individual Flower Essences

Candy Barrel Cactus 161

Cane Cholla Cactus 136, 163

Claret Cup Hedgehog Cactus 60

Desert Christmas Cholla Cactus 86

Desert Holly 163

Fairy Duster 161

Foothills Paloverde 86

Indian Root 86
Milky Nipple Cactus 127, 128, 163
Morning Glory Tree 163
Mullein 138
Queen of the Night Cactus 32, 86
Red Root 159
Saguaro Cactus 18, 28, 54
Sow Thistle 127, 129
Spineless Prickly Pear Cactus 192
Staghorn Cholla Cactus 18
Syrian Rue 136, 149
Teddy Bear Cholla Cactus 161
White Desert Primrose 133

—

Resources

Desert Alchemy® Flower Essences

See your local natural foods store, natural heath care supplier, alternative bookstore or contact us at:

Desert Alchemy, L.L.C.
P.O. Box 44189
Tucson, AZ 85733
Toll Free USA & Canada: (800) 736-3382
Tel: (520) 325-1545
Fax: (520) 325-8405
E-mail: info@desert-alchemy.com

Desert Alchemy® Web Site

For up to date information on classes, workshops and the latest research information, please visit Desert Alchemy's web site at *www.desert-alchemy.com*

Flower Essence Practitioner's Subscription Newsletter

Desert Alchemy publishes *Desert Voice*, a subscription newsletter presenting research and practical application of desert flower essences. It includes featured essences, healing themes, case histories, desert lore, questions and answers and more.

Flower Essence Consultations

Cynthia is available for consultations by appointment in person or by telephone. Special long-distance telephone rates are available to make international consultations possible.

Toll Free USA & Canada: (800) 736-3382
Tel: (520) 325-1545
Fax: (520) 325-8405
E-mail: consultations@desert-alchemy.com

About the Author

Cynthia Athina Kemp Scherer is an experienced flower essence practitioner, researcher, and the founder of Desert Alchemy. In 1983, while in the midst of a transformational life experience, she was inspired by nature to begin co-creating flower essences from the Arizona deserts. Her relationship to nature fostered deep healing experiences that provided the foundation for her years of research.

She lives in Tucson, Arizona, with her husband, and spends most of her time devoted to her practice, educational endeavors, and writing. She authors *Desert Voice*, a subscription flower essence practitioner's newsletter and other resource guides and books that highlight practical flower essence use. Cynthia and her husband continually develop Desert Alchemy's internet web site as a further educational resource.

Since 1986, one of Cynthia's great loves has been sharing in workshops about her experiences in using flower essences and her ever-deepening relationship with nature. She teaches at various schools, universities, and in workshop settings. She welcomes feedback, experiential stories and case histories using desert flower essences.

About the Photo on the Cover

Pictured on the cover is a Spineless Prickly Pear Cactus flower. Through its flower essence, this plant brings us an important support. How many of us want to change or heal a limitation we have but are convinced at some deep level that we won't be able? We often procrastinate, even when we know the first steps we need to take.

> *Often when this essence is indicated we feel as if we don't deserve something after all. We want something but we feel that we won't be able to have it. Our disappointment covers up procrastination. The real problem is in our motivation. We are not really motivated to go all out for what we want because we fear that we don't really deserve it. When we are challenged, we yield too easily to the difficulty of the challenge and give up. It is a convenient way of proving ourselves right; we really don't deserve to have what we want. This is the essence of choice for procrastination.*
>
> *Spineless Prickly Pear Cactus helps by showing us that whatever we have in front of us at any given moment is our tool, our way out of a problem or challenge. Instead of feeling defeated by a situation, we can use its challenge to our advantage.* [1]

This book could be one of your tools. The only way its five-step process won't work is if you don't use it.

---

1   *The Alchemy of the Desert*, Cynthia Athina Kemp Scherer, Desert Alchemy Editions, 1997.